THE IDENTITY TRAP

the identity trap
saving our teens
from themselves

JOSEPH NOWINSKI, PH.D.

AMACOM AMERICAN MANAGEMENT ASSOCIATION

New York • Atlanta • Brussels • Chicago • Mexico City • San Francisco
Shanghai • Tokyo • Toronto • Washington, D. C.

Special discounts on bulk quantities of AMACOM books are available to corporations, professional associations, and other organizations. For details, contact Special Sales Department, AMACOM, a division of American Management Association, 1601 Broadway, New York, NY 10019.
Tel.: 212-903-8316. Fax: 212-903-8083.
Web site: www. amacombooks.org

This publication is designed to provide accurate and authoritative information in regard to the subject matter covered. It is sold with the understanding that the publisher is not engaged in rendering legal, accounting, or other professional service. If legal advice or other expert assistance is required, the services of a competent professional person should be sought.

Library of Congress Cataloging-in-Publication Data

Nowinski, Joseph.
   Identity trap : saving our teens from themselves / Joseph Nowinski.
      p. cm.
   Includes bibliographical references and index.
   ISBN-13: 978-0-8144-7366-5
   ISBN-10: 0-8144-7366-0
   1. Parent and teenager. 2. Adolescent psychology. 3. Parenting. I. Title.

HQ799.15.N69 2007
649'.125—dc22

2006034253

Printing number
10 9 8 7 6 5 4 3 2 1

For Maggie, Becca, and Greg—
you are the sunshine of my life,
the apples of my eye.

CONTENTS

INTRODUCTION:
Saving Teens from Themselves

If your five-year-old son or daughter were to climb a tree to a height that made you anxious, an appropriate response might be, "Get down from that tree this minute!" On the other hand, if you find that your fifteen-year-old son or daughter has climbed a tree to a precarious height, a better response is, "Why are you in that tree?" Similarly, if your five-year-old throws a toy at a friend, an appropriate response might be, "Go sit in the corner!" On the other hand, if your fifteen-year-old throws a punch at someone, the better response would be, "Who do you think you are?" In this book, I will explain why this is so.

You will find that this book challenges you to let go of many ideas you may have about the best way to guide your teenager toward a happy and successful adulthood. It will help you to understand why the way you parented your child when he or she was in fact a child may actually work against you once he or she becomes an adolescent. The truth is that many of the things that seemed to be the natural, commonsense things to do when your children were toddlers and preteens turn out to be exactly the wrong things to do just a few years later. To effectively parent a teenager, you need to let go of the way you parented your child and move on to a new way of parenting your teen. The reasons, which will become clear as you read on, have to do with the fact that the ways teens develop is very different from the way younger children develop. Therefore, the parenting strategies that work best are also very different.

The key to letting go of old notions and moving on to a new perspective on parenting is to understand the most important developmental task facing every adolescent is the development of an *identity:* that inner sense of who we are, why we are here, what we stand for, and where our life is heading. Every adult has such an identity, though we may have forgotten that it formed when we were teenagers.

What determines the kind of adult your child will become— whether she or he will be happy, self-confident and successful, or depressed, underachieving and self-destructive—is the identity that he or she develops during adolescence. Once identity begins to crystallize, such things as the consequences of behavior—reward versus punishment, for example—begin to have less and less influence. This may seem counterintuitive, especially since you are probably accustomed to using consequences to control your child's behavior. Indeed, this may have worked when your child was a child, but, as most parents of teens quickly find out, rewards and punishments do not work as well with their teenage sons or daughters as they did just a few years earlier.

As your teenager's identity takes shape, that identity—more than simple external consequences—determines the way your child sees the world. This includes your teenager's attitudes, expectations, as well as how he or she acts. One way to think of identity is as a lens through which we view the world. Of course, you'd like your child's lens to be as rosy as possible. You'd like your child to see the world as a welcoming place, where cooperation and collaboration are recognized and valued; to see his or her future filled with possibilities; and to see him- or herself as a valued member of society.

Sadly, things don't always turn out that way. Many teens find themselves trapped in their own identity; that is, once they settle on a fixed view of themselves and the world they continue to act in ways that reflect that identity, until (and unless) their image of themselves changes. Problems such as drug abuse, chronic academic failure, difficulty getting peer acceptance, aggressiveness, self-mutilation, and so on, reflect the identities of teenagers who view themselves and the world through a dark lens and act accordingly.

It's important to understand that aggressive teenagers do not behave that way simply because they have been rewarded for being aggressive, rather they behave that way because being aggressive is consistent with their sense of who they are (tough people) and how they see the world (a tough place). On the other hand, a timid teenager behaves that way because she or he is embracing the identity of a weak and vulnerable person, although he or she has not been rewarded for being timid. And so on. To alter such behaviors as aggressiveness and timidity requires neither reward nor punishment; rather, it requires that you help your child see him- or herself in a different way—in other words, that you steer your teenager toward a healthier identity.

Although you cannot dictate precisely what identity your child will ultimately embrace, by understanding how your child's identity is formed you can create situations and relate to him or her in ways that will minimize the chances that your child will develop an identity that will lead to a life of unhappiness and failure. The good news, therefore, is that you can successfully address even serious problems such as eating disorders, self-destructiveness, depression, aggressiveness, and underachievement—if you understand what these behaviors mean, what needs to change, and how to promote those changes.

As a psychologist who has worked with teens and their families for more than two decades, I know this can be done, and that you can help your child do it, too. I have created this book to serve as your guide. To illustrate how teenagers develop their identities and the problems they encounter in the process, I have included many stories of adolescents, who have come close to embracing limiting, dysfunctional, or self-destructive identities, but who were guided back toward healthy ones. Though thoroughly disguised to protect their privacy, all of the cases discussed are based on real people. Working with them through their travails has enriched me and helped me to be a better parent. I am grateful to have had the opportunity to be a part of these individuals' lives, even briefly.

I provide advice on how to achieve this goal, using several simple tools:

- *Heads Up* highlights things to be sure to do, as well as things to watch out for.

- *Guiding Your Teen* . . . will take you through the process step by step and show you how to steer your teenager's search for identity in a healthy direction.

- *Exercises* designed to get you thinking creatively about parenting have been added at appropriate places in the text.

- *FAQs* at the end of each chapter provide answers to questions commonly asked by parents faced with the challenge of guiding a teen into a productive and happy adulthood.

I have also included an appendix, Fast FAQs Guide to Parenting Teens, that you can use as a handy reference or as food for thought.

ACKNOWLEDGMENTS

I would like to express my sincere appreciation to Linda Konner for keeping the faith and for her steady support over the years that she has represented me, and to my editor at Amacom, Ellen Kadin, whose unflagging enthusiasm for this writing project lifted me at times, and whose thoughtful commentary made this a better book. I also owe a debt of gratitude to Ellen Coleman for her careful editing of the manuscript, and for asking questions that helped me through some bumps in the road. I would like to express my admiration for David Van Rooy and Mark Thomson, whose work with children and teens at St. John's Home in Grand Rapids, Michigan, inspired me to organize my own thoughts about adolescent development and treatment, and to put them into words. Last, but not least, I wish to acknowledge my debt to Terri and to Emily for their exemplary parenting.

THE IDENTITY TRAP

1

how children act versus who they are

LET'S BEGIN OUR exploration of identity with a lesson from literature. George Bernard Shaw wrote a play titled *Pygmalion* (later made into a musical titled *My Fair Lady*). Shaw was a keen observer of people, and he had a good idea of what made us tick. In the play, Shaw offers important insights into how identity determines how we behave—as well as how we can influence our identities.

Pygmalion tells the story of a very interesting social experiment. Professor Henry Higgins, a dour teacher of linguistics, decides to pass off Eliza Doolittle, a young street urchin who earns her living selling flowers to passersby on the streets of London, as a "lady" in high society. The story begins when Eliza comes to Higgins's home seeking elocution lessons, believing that the only way she can do better in class-conscious London than selling flowers is by learning to speak better. On a bet with his friend Colonel Pickering, Higgins takes on the challenge not only of teaching her how to speak well, but also of converting the crude and raw Eliza into a genteel lady.

Eliza endures the grueling course of instruction under Higgins's severe tutelage. He sets his goal to teach her how to talk, walk, and act the part. He is demanding and critical, relentless and sarcastic, all in an effort to transform this flower girl and win his bet with his friend Pickering.

In the end, Higgins does succeed; Eliza performs gloriously at the embassy reception she attends with Higgins.

Afterward, however, Shaw shows us that it was Pickering, just as much as Professor Higgins, who has had an effect on Eliza. We learn that, while Higgins devoted himself exclusively to shaping Eliza's *behavior*, Pickering has in fact affected her *identity*. He accomplishes this feat by the way he relates to—acts and treats—Eliza. In the end, Eliza not only acts and speaks like a lady, but, perhaps more important, she *feels* like a lady. That is her new identity—an outcome for which Eliza credits Pickering more than Higgins.

Late in Shaw's play, Eliza, recognizing the change in her own identity, has the following talk with Colonel Pickering:

Eliza: Will you drop me altogether now that the experiment is over, Colonel Pickering?

Pickering: Oh don't. You mustn't think of it as an experiment.

Eliza: But I owe so much to you that I should be very unhappy if you forgot me.

Pickering: It's very kind of you to say so, Miss Doolittle.

Eliza: It's not because you paid for my dresses. I know you are generous to everybody with money. But it was from you that I learnt really nice manners; and that is what makes one a lady, isn't it? You see it was so very difficult for me with the example of Professor Higgins always before me. I was brought up to be just like him, unable to control myself, and using bad language on the slightest provocation. And I should never have known that ladies and gentlemen didn't behave like that if you hadn't been there.

Pickering: Oh, that's only his way, you know. He doesn't mean it.

Eliza: Oh, I didn't mean it either, when I was a flower girl. It was only my way. But you see I did it; and that's what makes the difference after all.

Pickering: No doubt. Still, he taught you to speak; and I couldn't have done that, you know.

Eliza: Of course: that is his profession. It was just like learning to dance in the fashionable way: there was nothing more than that in it. But do you know what began my real education?

Pickering: What?

Eliza: Your calling me Miss Doolittle that day when I first came to Wimpole Street. That was the beginning of self respect for me. And there were a hundred little things you never noticed, because they came naturally to you. Things like standing up and taking off your hat and opening doors—

Pickering: Oh that was nothing.

Eliza: Yes: things that showed you thought and felt about me as if I were something better than a scullery-maid; though I know you would have been just the same to a scullery-maid if she had been let into the drawing room. You never took off your boots in the dining room when I was there.

Pickering: You mustn't mind that. Higgins takes off his boots all over the place.

Eliza: I know. I am not blaming him. It is his way, isn't it? But it made such a difference to me that you didn't do it. You see, really and truly, apart from the other things anyone can pick up (the dressing and the proper way of speaking, and so on) the difference between a lady and a flower girl is not how she behaves, but how she's treated. I shall always be a flower girl to Professor Higgins, because he always treats me as a flower girl, and always will; but I know I can be a lady to you, because you always treat me as a lady, and always will.

What Were You Like as a Teen?

So there you have it: the difference between being a flower girl and a lady did not derive merely from sounding like a lady or acting like a lady; it came from *feeling* like a lady. It was not what Eliza was taught, but how she *was treated* that taught her this lesson! If this is true, might it not follow that the difference between a bully, an underachiever, a self-mutilator, or an alienated youth and an All-American kid may have a lot to do with the expectations we have for a child and the way we relate to that child? You can take a page from *Pygmalion* and learn to use it to guide your child through adolescence and toward the kind of healthy identity that Eliza ended up with; I'll show you how.

> **HEADS UP!** *Look beyond your child's behavior for the solution.*

By contrasting the importance of Higgins to that of Pickering, I am not suggesting that parents should abandon their role as teachers. I am saying that if you allow yourself to become like Higgins—to focus all your attention and efforts on simply monitoring and correcting behavior—you may be missing the forest for the trees. As Eliza correctly points out, it was Pickering who had the more profound and lasting effect on her.

You may have experienced something similar when you were a teen. Can you recall someone who influenced how you felt about yourself? How much of that was due to the way they related to you, as opposed to the power they may have had over you?

Always remember that identity determines behavior, not just rewards, punishments, criticism, or instruction. As an example, consider manners. Teaching children good manners is important. But manners are merely behavior, and it is entirely possible for a teenager (or an adult, for that matter) to display what may appear on the surface to be good manners, but which in reality is merely a show. Surely, you've known someone like that. Being a truly well-mannered person goes deeper than that. It reflects not only behavior, but an attitude behind that behavior that is made up of a combination of self-respect, kindness, and generosity. Teenagers who treat others with true courtesy do so not for show, or simply to impress others, but because they experience themselves as kind and caring people

Another example is the problem of anger. Teaching an adolescent with a history of aggression what is popularly called "anger management skills" can be useful, but only if that teen also comes to see him- or herself as a fundamentally nonviolent person; that is, if his or her identity shifts away from aggression and toward negotiation as a preferred way of dealing with conflict or frustration. Eric Harris and Dylan Klebold, the notorious Columbine High School shooters, had been required to attend anger management classes. They both passed. However, as we all know, they later shot and killed fellow students and a teacher before shooting themselves. Clearly, the anger management classes did not affect their underlying identities. In their writings, it is clear that they viewed themselves as alienated, venomously angry young men, and that this is what accounted for their behavior.

Teaching manners or anger management skills is useful only in so far as these things are compatible with an adolescent's developing identity. If you choose to focus all of your energy and attention on your child's behavior, and overlook the identity that is forming within, you could be in store for a lot of frustration and, possibly, heartbreak.

GLANCING BACKWARD TO MOVE FORWARD

Take a moment to reflect on your own childhood and adolescence and it will quickly become apparent that your emerging identity—your sense of who you were—was a much more powerful determiner of what you did or didn't do than any specific rewards or punishments you may have experienced. I'm not saying that you didn't like being rewarded (or dislike being punished), only that these consequences tend to have less influence on behavior once identity comes into play.

Exercise 1–1 will take only a few minutes, but it will help you come up with a thumbnail sketch of the identity that was forming inside of you when you were a teen.

Exercise 1–1: Who Were You When You Were a Teen?

For each of the following dimensions, make a mark at that point between the two extremes that best describes your sense of who you were:

Competitive ——————————— Noncompetitive

Athletic ——————————— Nonathletic

Aggressive ——————————— Docile

Rebellious——————————— Compliant

Confident——————————— Anxious

Social——————————— Loner

Risk-taker ——————————— Cautious

Popular ———————✓———————————— Unpopular

Attractive ——————✓————————————— Unattractive

Optimistic ———————————————✓——— Pessimistic

Adventurous —✓———————————————— Homebody

Strong —✓———————————————————— Frail

Special —✓———————————————————— Ordinary

Happy ———————————————————✓——— Sad

Energetic ——————————————————✓— Sedentary

Motivated ——————————————————✓—— Unmotivated

Creative ———————————————————✓— Uncreative

The characteristics included in the exercise are only a sampling of the number of dimensions you could use to describe your sense of who you were as a teen, so feel free to add others that apply. When you've completed Exercise 1–1, you will have a sense of the identity that was forming inside you when you were a teen. As you think about it, you may be able to connect that emerging identity with how you behaved, with your expectations for yourself, your goals and aspirations, and important decisions you made. Perhaps you saw yourself as a creative, adventurous, and competitive person, and this may have led you to try new things and take chances. Conversely, if you saw yourself as someone who was not particularly creative, uncompetitive in most situations, conservative, and cautious, you may have chosen to play it safe most of the time, regardless of whether that strategy really worked well and made you happy, or left you feeling empty and frustrated.

As you reflect on it, you may also see how your view of yourself along any of these lines was not fixed in concrete, but was something that evolved over time. Eventually, though, your view of yourself vis-à-vis each of these dimensions settled somewhere on the scale. Your teenage son or daughter now is where you were then; his or her identity is open to change.

Now complete Exercise 1–2.

Exercise 1–2: How Did You Evolve When You Were a Teen?
To complete this backward glance at yourself, answer the following questions:

1. Which of the dimensions listed in Exercise 1–1 changed over time during your own adolescence?

   - Which *experiences* had an influence on how you felt about yourself? Israel, college (art.)

   - Which *adults* had an influence on how you felt about yourself? Elaine (special, worthy of attention)

   - Which *peers* had the most influence on how you felt about yourself? Carolyn → saw the way I am

2. List three things you liked best about yourself when you were an adolescent. own compass re: destiny
   funny, liked

3. List three things you most criticized yourself for as an adolescent.
   - unattr.
   - didn't care about school
   - unable to generate dwellers

4. Looking back, which, if any, of these do you wish you could have changed in terms of how you felt about yourself?

   - Do you wish you had pursued some *activity* that you didn't?

   - Do you wish you'd pursued a *relationship* that you didn't? Art
   not really

5. Can you see how your behavior when you were a teen was

a reflection of your sense of your identity? Think of two or three examples of how your behavior or your expectations for yourself were determined primarily by how you felt about yourself.

6. How aware do you believe your parents were aware of your identity?

   ▪ Did you ever share your feelings about yourself with a parent?

   ▪ If you did, what kind of reaction did you get? If you didn't, what stopped you?

   ▪ Did your parents say anything about the kind of person they thought you were? How did their perception square with your private view of yourself?

7. Can you recall decisions you made that were influenced by your sense of who you were? What were they? Looking back, are there many decisions that you regret?

8. Finally, how does your current view of yourself as an adult compare to how you felt about yourself as a teenager? If it's different, what experiences or relationships contributed to this change in your identity?

Exercise 1–2 should have helped you focus on the role your emerging identity may have played on your choices and your behavior, and put you in a better position to see how similar things may be at work in your teen's life.

Let's begin with a description of one teen whose behavior makes sense only if you appreciate the role that identity plays in determining that behavior. As you read it, you may gain some insights into yours or your teenager's behavior, or, even, both.

Reality Check: Size-One Sally

Sally, at fifteen, was in that state of bursting out of childhood and into adulthood that most of us typically look back on with equal parts joy and terror. Tall and slender, she had dark wavy hair that she liked to wear in either a ponytail or cascading across her shoulders. She was an extremely articulate and remarkably observant teen. She had a flair for dressing in strikingly attractive ways, loved shopping, and was a devoted bargain hunter. Unfortunately, she was also in the midst of developing a dysfunctional, self-destructive identity.

Sally's parents first noticed her eating and exercise habits shortly after she turned fourteen, and it wasn't long before they became concerned. First, her mother noticed that Sally was becoming incredibly picky at meals and ate less and less. After meals she would retreat to her room, where she could be heard doing sit-ups for an hour or more. Then she ate nothing at meals, but, between meals, she would fill up on watermelon or saltines and peanut butter.

Although they noticed this behavior, Sally's parents were distracted from their daughter's eating habits by the troubles of her older brother, Tyler. A senior in high school, Tyler had been arrested for possession of marijuana. After a lengthy and expensive legal process, he was placed on probation. Between the drawn-out legal proceedings and the drug treatment that Tyler was subsequently mandated to attend, Tyler's parents were drained, financially and emotionally. So Sally—who, according to her parents had always been the happy, responsible, loving child—accidentally got shortchanged when it came to time and attention.

Sally was a good student, well-liked by her teachers and active in the school drama club and swim team. In many ways, she was the opposite of her brother, who though talented and articulate, had decided for some unknown reason at around age eight that he couldn't compete with the really smart kids. He'd been an underachiever ever since. The fact that he smoked marijuana regularly didn't help matters. By the time he was a teen, Tyler's identity seemed to be that of someone with great potential but few accomplishments, funny and easygoing but unreliable.

Sally's mother first tried talking to her about her weight and eating habits. She explained that both she and Sally's father were aware of how picky Sally was about what she ate, and how she would often do sit-ups after eating a meal. They believed she was trying to instantly burn off any calories she consumed. They also suspected that, at times, Sally was intentionally vomiting. Sally denied all of this and vigorously defended her eating habits, claiming they were no more extreme than those of any number of friends. She acknowledged that over the past year she had lost ten pounds (despite having grown more than an inch), but blew off her mother's concerns. Nevertheless, her mother persisted. She told Sally that friends and relatives had commented that she looked emaciated.

No matter how much her mother talked to Sally, nothing changed. The responses were always the same: Sally just wasn't hungry; she liked to exercise after she ate; she was no thinner than her friends; and so on.

Exasperated, Sally's mother finally brought her to their pediatrician, who confirmed that the girl was seriously underweight, and also discovered that Sally had not had a period in over six months. She referred Sally to a psychiatrist, who prescribed medication for depression (which, it turned out, Sally rarely took, fearing it would make her put on weight!) and referred Sally to a therapist.

The therapist approached the problem from the point of view of behavior. She asked Sally to keep a journal of all the food she ate, as well as how she was feeling day to day. The therapist weighed Sally at the outset of each session. She spent a lot of time talking to Sally about food, going over nutritional needs and the potential consequences of malnutrition, such as eventual osteoporosis and lasting disruption of her menstrual cycle. She tried to engage Sally in setting weight goals, and suggested in family sessions that Sally's parents tie these goals to some reward, like new clothes.

Sally nodded, but months went by and nothing changed. When Sally suddenly lost another two pounds in the span of a week, her therapist called for an emergency family session, and recommended that Sally be given mandatory weight-gain goals. If Sally failed to meet them, the therapist advised her parents to ground her from all after-school and weekend activities until she did; if she met or exceeded them, she would get extra privileges. The therapist warned that Sally might have to be hospitalized.

Things still did not get better, but neither did they get worse. As her weight hovered at 100 pounds, and she grew taller (five foot eight), Sally continued to maintain that she was not anorexic, but merely thin.

HEADS UP! Don't think "mental illness" as your first response to your teen's problems.

What to Do When You Suspect Your Child Is in Trouble

Perhaps you can relate to Sally's story. Maybe you suspect that your child has an eating disorder. Or, perhaps, the problem isn't with weight and eating, but something else your son or daughter is doing that makes you wake up in the middle of the night. The way your child is behaving just doesn't make sense to you, but trying to talk to him or her about it gets you nowhere. Maybe you've brought your child to see a physician, or a psychiatrist, who suggested medication. This is a strong trend in America today. We are diagnosing and medicating teens in ever-increasing numbers. Parents agree to this because their child's behavior doesn't make sense to them, because they want him or her to be happy and successful, and because they don't know what else to do. Often, though, all this process of diagnosis and medication accomplishes is to build a bigger wall between parents and their children. That's what Sally's parents did, despite their best intentions.

You can deal with your concerns in a different way.

When I met with Sally I naturally noticed how thin she was—it was impossible not to—but I made a point of not making this the first thing I asked her about. Neither did I steer the conversation toward nutrition, nor sermonize about the possible consequences of anorexia or bulimia on her long-term health. I knew what I'd have done as a teenager if a doctor or other authority figure tried to lecture me. I might have said nothing, but I'd have tuned it out, and surely wouldn't have been motivated to open up about what my life was really like.

> **HEADS UP!** *Stay off the soapbox.*

Your teen's behavior reflects his or her emerging identity, and learning about that identity is more useful than focusing on behavior. By challenging your child's behavior directly, you are in effect challenging his or her identity. Imagine how you'd feel if, the first time we met, I asked you why you behaved the way you do, implying that I disapproved of it? I am not saying that you should simply ignore behavior that worries you. Of course, you should point it out and ask about it. However, don't fall into the trap of making worrisome behavior the only topic of conversation, don't constantly question it or lecture your teen about it. That strategy will only make things worse. One clever set of parents actually built a soapbox, which they kept in a corner of the family room. Whenever someone felt that someone else was "getting on a soapbox," that person could hand the box to the speaker.

If you think of your child's behavior as something that is driven by his or her emerging identity, then you may choose a different path, and instead try to gain some insight into what that developing identity is. From there you may be able understand why your teenager's behavior makes sense to them, even if it does not to you. This, in turn, will open the door to further communication, which is what you want.

OPEN THE DOOR TO REAL COMMUNICATION

Using the above strategy, I avoided talking about nutrition, weight, and eating and expressed great interest instead in things like Sally's activities, her social life and relationships, and her interest in fashion. I shared my surprise when she told me that she'd been thinking about dropping off the high school swim team for the coming season. I briefly shared with Sally a couple of my own experiences with sports—the good and the bad—and then expressed my interest in knowing more about Sally's interests, her taste in books and music, who her best friends were, who she disliked (and why), and what the issues were in her life from her point of view. In other words, I focused very little on Sally's problem behavior, and instead tried to get some to know what it was like to be Sally.

> **HEADS UP!** *Begin a dialogue with your teenager that will last forever.*

Although Sally outwardly presented an image of a happy, care-free girl, I soon learned that her world was actually fraught with challenges, conflicts, and threats, of which her parents were not even dimly aware. For beginners, her high school was a place where most kids at least experimented with alcohol and drugs— "Just about everybody drinks and smokes pot," she told me—and it was considered uncool to be "straight-edge," meaning alcohol- and drug-free. The latest fad in drug use was pharmaceuticals, especially medications for attention deficit, painkillers, and tranquilizers. Sally had experimented with pot a few times, and had gotten drunk a number of times. She'd had sex one time in that state, and didn't feel good about it, and narrowly averted what might have been a dangerous situation when she got into a car with three drunk boys, only one of whom she knew. Fortunately, she was just sober enough to realize where she was and exited the car while the boys were still getting in.

Bullying, which occurred among girls as well as boys, was another problem in Sally's world, even though she lived in a solidly middle-class community. Several of her friends had already had scuffles with other girls that year, though all had managed to get out of them before actual punches were thrown. These encounters were over such issues as competing for boyfriends, or another girl's "attitude." Each year, more students were arrested for assault or drug possession.

Sally referred to the main in-group in her school as the "Abercrombies"—boys and girls who owned large wardrobes of designer label clothes, drove new or relatively new cars, and had money to burn. A few Abercrombies were athletes, and this select group occupied the top of the social food chain.

In Sally's view, the typical Abercrombie girl was vain, competitive, and mean, and although she actually was friends with a couple of them, she was not part of their clique. Though Sally's parents were not poor, she neither had—nor especially wanted to have—the material possessions that every Abercrombie coveted.

Sally generally liked boys. She had a number of boy "friends," but no boyfriend, and had no strong desire to commit to a relationship or be sexual. In fact, she was determined to stop drinking before she got drunk, in order to avoid a second random sexual encounter; this set her apart from many of her friends, who slept around quite a bit. On the other hand, Sally was deeply frustrated with a close friend who was glued to a new boyfriend, which meant that Sally hardly saw her.

HEADS UP! *Open your ears; close your mouth.*

To put it bluntly, if you want to engage your son or daughter in productive rather than frustrating conversations, begin by trying to do much more listening than talking and avoid offering unsolicited advice. (Remember your own adolescence—how much unasked for advice would you have heeded?) Your reward will be a great deal of insight into your child's world, which is the crucible from which his or her identity will emerge. It's hard to resist telling your teenage son or daughter what you think ought to done—in effect, from jumping into your child's life in an attempt to change them. It's understandable, but it doesn't work.

This, then, was the real world in which Sally lived. Her parents had little idea of what that world was like—not because they didn't care about her, but because they focused almost exclusively on her behavior, especially the behavior that worried them. Like most parents, Sally's were preoccupied with eliminating that behavior. But the more their relationship with Sally revolved around her behavior, the more she resisted, and the greater the distance between them became.

HEADS UP! *Get a glimpse into the world your teen inhabits.*

Adolescents in America live in what amounts to a secret society. You can gain some insight into this secret society if you take time to watch the television shows and listen to the music that your kids do. At best, however, this will be a very limited view. To really understand your teenagers, it's important to put aside your anxiety and any preoccupation you may have with changing their behavior, and instead get them to actually describe their worlds. Only then can you guide them toward a healthy identity.

Sally—just like your teen—was actively searching for an identity. From where she stood, her eating habits and almost everything she did, made perfect sense. Once I learned that Sally's friends' had nicknamed her "Size-One Sally," it made sense to me, too. It was a joke at first, a bit of friendly teasing, but something about the moniker struck a chord in Sally the very first time she heard it. She now thought of herself that way; indeed, she was proud to be "Size-One Sally." It was becoming a core part of her identity. From Sally's perspective she was engaged in a struggle for perfection: to be totally fat-less and able to fit into the slimmest clothing on the rack. Because her parents did not know that her size was central to their daughter's emerging identity, they felt they had to challenge her, and to interpret her behavior as a symptom of mental illness.

> **HEADS UP!** *Get off on the right foot—don't be judgmental.*

Assuming you are successful and open communication does lead to some insight into your child's emerging identity, it is vital that you avoid communicating rejection of that identity in any way. Criticizing or challenging what you sense is your teen's emerging identity usually shuts down the very communication that you need to maintain in order to help them when *they are ready* for that help.

This is important because, like adults, teens heed advice only when they ask for it. You can influence your child's identity development, but not by attacking it or criticizing it.

SUGGEST MEANINGFUL ALTERNATIVES

For example, Sally offhandedly remarked that she knew she was obsessed with her weight and eating. Sometimes it bothered her to be the only one agonizing over a menu, and sometimes when her friends would notice her agony and laugh, she was embarrassed. Given this opening, I responded to Sally's revelation. "I can see how that would be embarrassing. I can also see how being Size-One Sally is becoming a part of your identity. Of course, there are many other identities to choose from, and maybe some day you will decide you want to be more than Size-One Sally, or even give that identity up for a totally different one. Given your talents and abilities, I'm sure that if you decide to look at all the available alternatives, you will settle on an identity that you can be proud of."

> **HEADS UP!** Introduce the idea of choice.

You can guide your child toward a healthy identity by accepting their current sense of who they are and, when opportunities arise, simply letting them know that they have choices, but don't try to steer them in a particular direction, or they may very well head the other way! Just emphasize, as often as you can, your belief that they have choices about who they are, the opportunities that are available to them, and the direction their life can take.

Sally was far from a hopeless case, but she was showing signs of embracing an identity that was dangerous to her health. (I get even more concerned when I see an adolescent who is trying on an identity as a "druggie" or an "outsider." These are real identities in the world of adolescents and unlike being an Abercrombie, which has its drawbacks in terms of materialism and snobbery, they are not very functional in the adult world; being an Abercrombie, on the other hand, is an identity that can at least lead to an acceptable niche in adulthood.)

Sally's declining interest in previously rewarding activities like swimming was another concern. Still, she had a lot going for her, including intelligence, wit, popularity, and good looks, the fact that her grades were good, and that she had a more or less positive outlook for the future.

> **HEADS UP!** *Keep a balanced perspective.*

As concerned as you may be about your child's behavior, try to keep a balance in your mind between what they do that worries you or gets them into trouble and their personal assets and talents. This can help you keep your own anxiety in check and allow you to relate to your child in a more optimistic, upbeat way.

SALLY TODAY

Too often, books on parenting describe the problems that youths face in great detail, but say little about how the stories they begin end. I follow the teens and families I work with periodically, and stay in touch with them for as long as they wish. Happily, Sally now plans to go to college after she graduates from high school at the end of this year. She's maintained a good grade point average, and is on the varsity swim team. She remains slim, but no one would call her emaciated any more. She thinks that she might want to become a fashion designer or graphic artist. Her prognosis is good for creating a healthy identity that will guide her to a satisfying life as an adult is good, and that's the best outcome of adolescence that a parent can hope for.

Guiding Your Teen . . . To a Healthy Identity

Sally is a good example of a teenager on the verge of a steep decline that could affect the quality of her present life as well as her future prospects if she continues to build an identity that limits rather than allows her to realize her considerable potential. If your child is like Sally, how can you save him or her from that fate?

If I succeed in making only one point in this chapter, I would want it to be how important it is to understand that the way your teenager *behaves* can be a window onto their emerging sense of who they *are*. You need to be able to see your child's behavior as a reflection of an emerging identity, which, for teens, is a work-in-progress. The more formed that identity becomes, the more it determines how your teen behaves. Viewed from your son or daughter's point of view, their behavior is not self-destructive, crazy, or dysfunctional.

FIVE GUIDELINES TO HELP YOU FOCUS ON IDENTITY, NOT JUST BEHAVIOR

Guideline #1: Don't try to impose your will. This is by far the hardest advice for a parent to follow. We are accustomed to trying to control our kids' behavior. When they are young, this works pretty well, and, in fact, it is often necessary to set limits and enforce them. However, this doesn't work very well for adolescents, who are in the process of developing an identity that may set their goals and drive their behavior for the rest of their lives. You need to recognize and respect this process of identity development.

Guideline #2: Treat your teen like the person you believe she or he can be. It never ceases to amaze me that it's possible to take a group of the most difficult teenagers in a treatment program to a Starbucks and watch them behave as though they were at a meeting of the local Chamber of Commerce. I think it's because the staff at Starbucks treats them as though they were customers, not disturbed teenagers.

Although your adolescents may still be children to you, and problem children at that, they no longer are children—nor are they fully formed adults. Their identity is still developing and has not yet crystallized; there is still time for it to change. Therefore, as frustrated, disappointed, and angry as you may be, try not to relate to your troublesome son or daughter as a loser, a failure, or a delinquent. Instead, try to keep in mind an image of what you believe your child can be, treat him or her with dignity and respect. Imagine that you are raising an All-American-child-in-the-rough and that what you see before you is not yet the finished product.

Guideline #3: Name the behavior. I've found it useful in my work with teens to talk openly about the idea that they are searching for an identity. That makes sense to them, especially if you let them know that you both understand and respect that process. Try saying something like "I understand that you are figuring out who you are," to communicate that you understand what's going on, and what's at stake in adolescence. Putting a name to the identity that goes with your child's behavior can help you curb any urge you may have to force a change in that behavior.

Guideline #4: Share your own teenage struggles. Give some thought to what you went through as an adolescent. If the previous exercises helped jog your memory, you may be able to recall how self-conscious you were, how sensitive you were to how others related to you, what you felt was best about yourself, and what about yourself worried you most. You might be able to recall whether the future looked bright and open or whether it seemed cloudy and uncertain. You might even be able to remember whether you had an image, or vision, of what your future might hold.

Guideline #5: Reserve judgment. The best way to get people to describe what their world and life is like is to be an interested interviewer, not someone looking to cast judgment. Most of us when we were teenagers did not let our parents know much about what our lives were like. In the world as it is, it is even riskier for you than it was for your parents to live in such ignorance. When it comes to talking with your teenage son or daughter, think of yourself as an anthropologist. Anthropologists describe a culture by observing it, but they do not try to influence or change it. As a therapist working with teens, I find that showing genuine interest without making judgment of any kind usually opens the door to insights into the richness and complexity of their lives. These insights usually let me get a grasp on the identity that is forming within any teenager. Whatever I find, and however it makes me feel, I try to avoid giving a teen the message that I think they're wrong or crazy, because if I do, my window onto that teen's identity will quickly close. If I remain "message-free," I find it is possible to influence identity. You can do this, too, but only if you don't directly challenge or criticize their current vision of reality too strongly.

These guidelines are a starting point to help you better understand your teenager and, ultimately, put yourself in a position to guide him or her toward a healthy identity. As much as you can influence this process, though, you also have to accept the fact that you can't totally control it. In fact, the more you try to control the process of identity formation—like the parents who are determined that their son or daughter will become a doctor—the more likely things are to go awry. People who work in institutions that have a reputation for shaping character, such as military academies, understand this. They know that you can only shape someone who is a willing participant in the process. In the past, many so-called "problem children" voluntarily enlisted in the armed services, and became successful citizens. Children who succeed in military academies must on some level desire the outcome. If they don't, they inevitably drop out or are kicked out. By respecting your child's ability to make choices and recognizing the right to determine the course of his or her life, you will be in a much better position to have influence than any coercive efforts, bribing, or nagging could achieve.

FAQs

Q: You say that I should focus on identity rather than on behavior. Does that mean I should just ignore whatever my teenager does? Wouldn't that be irresponsible?

A: A parent cannot afford to simply go along with whatever a teenager does; that would be irresponsible. However, focusing more or less exclusively on behavior often turns you into a "police officer," which usually leads to ongoing tension and further limits communication. It can tempt your child to continually test the limits and lead you to become obsessed about everything your teen does. I recommend setting reasonable limits, which will help you avoid getting caught up in trying to overcontrol your son or daughter. Step back and see if you can get a glimpse into how your teenager sees him or herself; the behavior may begin to make sense to you.

Q: What's the difference between "setting limits" and "imposing my will" on my teenager?

A: Setting limits is like putting a fence around your property and telling your child that he or she isn't allowed to go beyond that fence. When you erect the fence, you explain that it is there for safety reasons. You are not telling your child how he or she should act, or who he or she should be. Within the boundaries defined by the fence, your child is free to explore the world and learn about him- or herself. Imposing your will, on the other hand, is more than enforcing a boundary; it is dictating who your child should be.

Q: Am I just being naive if I treat my child like the person I believe he or she can be?

A: Not at all. A useful analogy is what typically happens to teens placed in an institution for treatment or diverted to an alternative school. The biggest determinant of how teens will act in those situations is the way they are treated. If they perceive that the staff see them as "problem kids" and expect problems, or as unintelligent and unmotivated students, then they will act that way. In contrast, if they perceive that the staff thinks of them as normal teens, who can control their behavior and succeed in school, then they will live up to those expectations. As difficult and maddening as your teenager may be at times, it's important to convey that you truly believe in his or her capacity to succeed and be happy.

Q: How much should I disclose about my own struggles in life, especially if I've had experiences of being abused?

A: It depends on how you think about your own experiences. If you still feel depressed and bitter about the bad things that happened to you, then you might communicate a certain amount of self-pity or hopelessness. However, if that's how you feel, you've probably already communicated that in some way. On the other hand, if you can tell your story so that it shows how it is possible to overcome adversity and lead a meaningful life, sharing your personal history can be very valuable to your teen.

2

It's not where your child has been, it's where he or she is going

IT IS IMPORTANT to balance an understanding of the past with an appreciation of the vital importance of the present and the future. Parents (and therapists) sometimes fall into the trap of thinking that the "cure" for a teen's problems, from depression and self-injurious behavior to drug abuse and aggression, is to be found in some kind of analysis of the past.

Although the past is relevant, from my point of view it is important only insofar as it helps us to understand what kinds of experiences may have influenced a teen's emerging identity. It's more important, however, to keep in mind that teens generally do not like to dwell on the past. Almost invariably, they say that dwelling on the past makes them feel depressed and hopeless. They are, rightly, much more concerned with what is happening to them now, and what their future looks like. Also, their identities are works in progress. That means that while they may have been influenced by past experiences, they are still open to influence in the here and now. And that's good news.

To guide your child toward a healthy identity, you need to help him or her keep his or her eye on the present and the future. You need to do your best to steer your child toward experiences that offer opportunities for success and the promise of a productive and meaningful adulthood.

Reality Check: Reckless Ryan

Ryan's mother was an accountant, his father a former engineer turned teacher. When Ryan was four years old, his younger brother, Eric, was born. That pregnancy had been difficult; Ryan's mother was confined to bed for the last month of it, and due in part to a bout of post-partum depression she had to take an extended leave from work afterward.

Not long after his mother returned to work, Ryan's father, an engineer specializing in information technology, fell on hard times when the corporation he worked for outsourced his entire department. The loss of income strained the family. Seeing no future in his former career, Ryan's father returned to school to become a teacher, and worked any job he could to make ends meet.

Although they couldn't afford luxuries for a few years, the family managed to keep their house and weather the financial storm. By then Ryan was seven and was living a comfortable life in a nice suburban neighborhood. From his parents' perspective, all was now right with the world and their family.

■ ■ ■

Ryan, now sixteen, shares a tier with fourteen other boys in the county jail, one of more than a hundred youths incarcerated there. Nearly half of them, like him, are from middle-class suburban and exurban communities. Each cell measures six by ten feet and features a combination toilet/sink made entirely of stainless steel, a metal frame bed thirty inches wide by sixty inches long that is bolted to the floor, and a narrow, barred window that seems impervious to even the slightest breeze on a hot summer day. The door is solid steel and slides open and shut by remote control from a glass-enclosed guard station. It has a small window, made of thick Plexiglas, which is drilled through about a dozen times with tiny holes through which Ryan and a passing guard may speak to each other.

Many of the youths on Ryan's tier spend most of their time watching television or listening to music. Others sleep as much as they can. Ryan has neither a television nor a radio to distract him. His parents can't afford to send him money to purchase them, because they spent most of their savings on an attorney to represent him. Ryan spends most of his time reading paperbacks that he gets from the jail's library.

> **HEADS UP!** Never allow yourself to become complacent.

Ryan's parents were shocked when they got that first call from a police officer telling them that their son had been arrested. They were aware, of course, of their son's problems in school. Still, their initial response was, "This can't be happening! Not to us! We're a middle-class family!" The truth is that situations like Ryan's are increasingly common in families just like Ryan's. Jails today house thousands of middle-class youths who are there for reasons such as drug possession, assault, and threatening behavior. If your child has been lucky so far, count yourself fortunate, but don't dismiss Ryan's story as something that could never happen in your family. Believing "it can't happen to us" is dangerous. Don't allow yourself to be lulled into a false sense of security.

Ryan's history of problem behavior goes back to fifth grade. He'd never particularly liked school. He always felt he had to struggle more that most of his friends just to get passing grades. Reading did not come easily to him, which caused him to fall further and further behind. By the time he was ten, Ryan had begun to gravitate toward the nonachievers in his class. Worse, thinking of himself as a "dummy" was becoming part of his sense of who he was. Once he began moving toward that identity, it drove his decisions, set his expectations, determined his motivation, and shaped his life. Ironically, in jail Ryan reads anything he can get his hands on, no matter how slowly he reads or how many times he has to reread it.

> **HEADS UP!** Keep your eyes and ears open for signs of academic frustration or a dislike of school that is becoming chronic.

What to Do When Your Child's Behavior Is Out of Control

Adolescents begin to carve out an identity based on their experiences and their perception of the options that are available to them. However, as Ryan's case illustrates, this process can actually begin much earlier. Factors that influence youngsters on the verge of forming an identity include the adults they look up to and admire, their early experiences with success and failure, how peers relate to them, and the opportunities and alternatives that they believe are open to them. You cannot control all of these things, but you should at least be aware of how important they are, and do what you can to see that your child has positive experiences, sees the future optimistically, does not feel hopeless, and believes that you respect him or her. You can't raise your child in a bubble, but you may be able to make sure his or her life is full of possibilities. In Ryan's case, you can see how his frustrating experiences in school, his drift toward an underachieving and unmotivated peer group, and finally landing in jail all combine to push him toward an unhealthy sense of himself that will determine what he does in the future.

Although Ryan never liked school and didn't do well in it, he didn't start having real problems until seventh grade, when he started skipping school and drinking liquor after school. His parents noticed that he was becoming increasingly moody, argumentative, and withdrawn, but, because they did not know about his drinking, they were unable to connect the dots.

When Ryan was punished for leaving school, typically with in-school suspensions, he'd simply walk out a back door and head for the house of a boy whose parents, like Ryan's, both worked. This meant that he and his friend—and sometimes others—were unsupervised and spent their time playing video games, drinking, and occasionally getting high on pot.

Finally, the school suggested that Ryan see a psychiatrist, who diagnosed him as defiant and depressed, with an attention-deficit disorder, and put him on several medications. Ryan passively accepted these diagnoses but took his medications only sporadically. He never revealed to either the doctor or his parents that he was drinking four or five days a week, and getting high another two or three times.

When I met him, there was nothing hostile, or even aggressive, that I could see about Ryan. He was, however, reckless, never stopping to think about the possible consequences of his actions. He was the classic tall, dark, and handsome youth, yet he typically preferred to blend into the background. His parents saw him in much the same way—a fundamentally gentle but rather lost soul, a kid without goals, who couldn't identify his talents or interests (other than video games), and a follower rather than a leader.

> **HEADS UP!** *When you can't connect the dots, consider the possibility of drugs or alcohol.*

Think long and hard about whether your youngster's behavior might be the result of alcohol or drugs. Regular use of alcohol or drugs leads to moodiness, depression, distractibility, lack of motivation, and general irritability; this pack of symptoms is often misdiagnosed as "mental illness" and treated with medication. Kids using drugs or getting drunk sometimes don't show up at school or home. Even without alcohol or drugs, teens are often moody (remember yourself as a teenager?). Drugs just make it worse. In addition, teens like Ryan have admitted to me that they would sooner accept a psychiatric diagnosis than own up to their alcohol or drug use. The trend today is increasingly toward the use of prescription medications, especially tranquilizers, stimulants, and painkillers, all of which can turn a teen's life into an emotional roller coaster. The best way to test any suspicion you may have about alcohol or drug use is to ask about it directly, as often as necessary, or suggest your child take a drug test (easily available over the counter in most drug stores). Explain that you are concerned about the emotions or behavior you're seeing, and that taking the test will lift a burden from your mind. It is your right and responsibility to do this, just as it is your right to have your child tested for Lyme disease if he or she is showing symptoms. In either case, a negative result will be a relief and help diminish any tension between you and your child.

Ryan's arrest was a direct result of drinking and drug abuse. He didn't know it, but he had inherited a vulnerability to alcoholism, which meant that when Ryan began drinking, he went very quickly from experimentation to being unable to stop until he either passed out or blacked out. Ryan's addiction had progressed so far that he could down a pint of vodka before either of these things would occur.

Ryan was arrested was for breaking and entering and also charged with resisting arrest—charges that could lead to a year or more in jail. Drunk, high, and trying to walk home in the middle of the night, he had stumbled on an unlocked van, climbed inside, and fell asleep while he was in a blackout. Hearing noises in his driveway, the homeowner called the police, who tried to arrest Ryan. Unfortunately, he was still in a blackout state and tried to run away.

The judge mandated Ryan to a drug treatment program and postponed further action until he completed it. Ryan was also diverted from his regular high school to an alternative high school operated by the school district. In family therapy sessions, it was recommended that Ryan's parents tie privileges to responsibilities. If Ryan skipped school, for example, he was to be grounded for three days, meaning that he could not go out or use his cell phone. On the other hand, if he attended school and got passing grades, his parents would continue to pay for his cell phone, and he would be allowed weekend overnight visits with friends.

Ryan's parents also brought him to individual therapy sessions, where Ryan found the conversation consistently steered toward his mother's depression, and to his father's experience with being laid off. The therapist repeatedly referred to these as "traumatic experiences," and it was soon clear to Ryan that the therapist saw some connection between them and his current situation. True to form, Ryan didn't object. But neither did he change.

HEADS UP! *Focus on the here and now!*

If your child is seeing a therapist, and if that therapist is preoccupied with talking about the past or intent on identifying a traumatic event in order to explain what's gone awry, you may want to consider a different form of therapy. The past may matter, but your child lives and will live in the present and the future. Ryan's mother's depression and his dad's layoff were facts, but they were not the reason Ryan was failing in school or was an alcoholic. On the contrary, his chronic frustration in school combined with the consequences of his alcoholism that were shaping his sense of himself and his view of what his future would hold. These factors, not family traumas, were progressively crystallizing Ryan's identity as a "loser."

Nothing can change the past. Losses can be mourned. Fears associated with frightening experiences can be acknowledged. Unfair treatment can be regretted. But there is little to be gained from being stuck on these things. Contrariwise, once you have a clue to the identity your child is forming and begin shifting your attention to what that identity could be many options will present themselves. That's what Ryan's parents learned to do. They made a sustained effort to present him with alternatives, and to expose him to situations that could challenge his negative image of himself.

HOW TO FOSTER A POSITIVE SELF-IMAGE

To be sure, Ryan was in a difficult spot. As you come to understand more about where identity comes from, and the crucial role it plays in your child's behavior, you will be able to see how you can influence things for the better. As painful as it was for everyone in the family, Ryan's arrest turned out to be wake-up call not only for him, but also for his parents. It was only then that they were able to see beyond the surface—Ryan's problem behavior—and realize that something was definitely going awry inside their son. That "something inside" (a dysfunctional identity in progress) was what was responsible for his behavior.

In jail, Ryan found himself surrounded by boys who were very obviously regarded as losers by most of those whose job it was to supervise them. Not a few were "throwaway" kids, kids who'd never had parents who loved them, or a stable place to live, or known any of the advantages that Ryan had. The friends Ryan made in the alternative school were only likely to lead him further down the path toward an antisocial identity—boys and girls who were mostly alienated or lost, full of anger or self-hatred. Left alone in this peer group, and with a pessimistic outlook for the future, Ryan's identity as a dummy and a loser was all the more likely to crystallize.

> **HEADS UP!** *Find out where your teen stands on the adolescent totem pole.*

You may find it difficult to believe that words like "dummy" or "loser" actually represent an identity, but they can and do. Ask your teenager to name the major groups in his or her school; they play a role in the formation of each student's identity. In Columbine High, for example, where Erik Harris and Dylan Klebold were students, students were broadly separated into two groups. Jessica Hughes, also a student at Columbine, described it this way: "There are basically two classes of people. There's the low and the high. The low sticks together and the high sticks together, and the high makes fun of the low and you just deal with it." Obviously, every teen at Columbine High knew which group he or she belonged to—where he or she fit in on this social totem pole. The same is true for your teenager. Try to learn which group your child believes he or she belongs to. If you are careful not to cast judgments, you'd be surprised how willing teens are to discuss their social world. Ask open-ended questions like the following to facilitate this kind of enlightening discussion:

- I'm curious about the different cliques in your school. Can you tell me about them?

- So, what groups are on the top of the food chain in your school? Who's on the bottom?

- Is there a social ladder of some sort in your school? How is it organized?

- Who are the most popular kids in school? What makes them popular?

- Is there much bullying or intimidation that goes on in school?

- Where do you see yourself fitting in at school?

- What do you think others think of you in school?

RYAN TODAY

Today, Ryan is in his second year at a local community college. He lives at home and works part-time. His relationship with his parents and his brother are greatly improved, and he has a girlfriend—someone he's known since first grade, but was too insecure to approach before. Luckily, shortly after he returned to the regular high school, she approached him, and he was confident enough to respond to her attention, instead of shying away.

Guiding Your Teen . . . To Positive Identity Choices

The process of change for Ryan—the way out of his identity trap—began when we first learned to see the world through his eyes. His parents and I did this by listening to the stories he told about his experiences over the past several years. As this picture emerged, his lack of motivation in school began to make sense, as did his drifting toward less achieving kids with whom he did not have to compete.

By pointing out the role that alcohol and drugs had played in his recent troubles, we were able to show Ryan that that was only one of many directions that his life could go in, and demonstrate that he still had *choices*—a message that he had not yet heard. Getting him appropriate academic help, including developing a relationship with a consistently positive academic coach, who showed him that he *could* learn, was part of the path leading the way out of the trap he'd fallen into.

FIVE GUIDELINES TO HELP YOUR TEEN MAKE HEALTHY CHOICES

Some of the specific things that can help a teen like Ryan move toward a healthier identity and a more optimistic future include the following:

Guideline #1: Give your child credit for having an inner drive to find an identity. You need to be frank with your teenager about the fact that he or she is an adolescent, and that adolescence is all about a search for identity. Signal that you don't want to tell your child who he or she should be, but that you understand that this search is going on and that you are willing to listen and be a sounding board any time he or she wants to "think out loud."

Guideline #2: Be optimistic about the future. No matter how frustrated or unhappy your child may seem, always communicate the idea that things can change. Don't negate what your teenager feels. Let your child know that when you were a teen, you had similar feelings at times. As bleak as things may seem, encourage your adolescent not to give up or surrender. In words or through your actions, strive to consistently give your teen the message that "it isn't where a person has been that really matters; it's where he or she is going."

Guideline #3: Introduce the concept of choice. Don't just introduce it; harp on it! It isn't hard to imagine why Ryan felt that his life was out of his control—that he was like a log drifting (if not sailing!) down a river. Many teens never get the message that they have a choice in the identity they embrace, and therefore in the direction their lives will go. Consistently talk about choice in a way that conveys that no matter how dire it seems, you truly believe your child's present situation can be turned around

Guideline #4: Identify strengths and expose them to success. Dysfunctional identities often have their roots in rejection, abuse, frustration, or other experiences that communicate failure rather than success. Imagine what it would be like to be a freshman at a high school and realize that you were lumped in with the lows or the losers. What would that do to your sense of self and your outlook on the future? How would it affect your motivation?

In addition to believing that you had choices, it would help to feel that you were in fact successful and talented. I have seen teens turn away from a dysfunctional identity simply by discovering a talent they didn't know they had. The best way to do this for your child is to create an environment that is rich in opportunities for new experiences. Think of parenting in part as an adventure to share with your children.

Guideline #5: Encourage your teen to make decisions. The first major change for Ryan came when he announced that he'd *decided* he didn't want to stay in the alternative school. By then his attendance had improved, and he was no longer drinking or smoking pot. He actually welcomed the random drug tests that his parents administered about every two weeks, because he had come to see them as on his side, wanting him to succeed and cheering him on, and he knew that alcohol and pot would sabotage all that. His grades were also improving, albeit slowly.

The next change came when Ryan said he'd *decided* he wanted to get extra help with schoolwork because of his learning disability. He'd always thought of himself as more or less dumb, and permanently handicapped because of his slow reading and difficulty retaining information. He'd never wanted to talk about it much within the family, mostly because his brother, in comparison, was an academic superstar; eventually Ryan did speak about how frustrated he'd been those first years in school. We talked about what he could do about it, if he *decided* he wanted to do something about it. Eventually he said he'd *decided* to seek extra help, but he wanted to do this at the regular high school, not the alternative school. Because of his good attendance record, the school administration agreed. They introduced him to a male history teacher who enjoyed working with teens who wanted to succeed. He became Ryan's academic "coach" as well as a respected mentor.

Think about your own life and some of the more important decisions you have made. How did it make you feel about yourself to be able to make decisions about your own life? Chances are that, like Ryan, you found this made you feel powerful and in control. It made you feel the opposite of depressed, the opposite of hopeless, and the opposite of adrift. These are the essential qualities of a functional identity; that is, one that is likely to lead to a life characterized by a sense of satisfaction and happiness. The more often we encourage teens to make decisions, and place our faith in their capacity to make them, the more we support the basics of healthy identity development.

FAQs

Q: Most professionals seem to say that children's and teens' problem behaviors are rooted in past experiences; are you saying that the past is insignificant?

A: It's not insignificant; I just don't believe that it is always as important as it is cracked up to be. Research on trauma suggests that more critical than whether or not a person is exposed to negative experiences is how the person reacts to them, which is why it is so important that you show your child how to react to them. If you react to difficult, painful experiences as if they will leave permanent scars and will limit your ability to be successful and happy, then expect your child to do the same. On the other hand, if you believe that life always throws some curve balls, and that you can recover even from traumatic experiences, then your child will believe and act that way as well. Recent research strongly supports the idea that many youths and adults experience so-called traumas with no discernable aftereffect.

Q: If that's true, then what role do past experiences play in identity development?

A: Past experiences are important to the extent that they communicate expectations for what a child may become. You can help by keeping the lines of communication open between you and your adolescent, so that you can keep an eye on how she or he is interpreting day-to-day experiences, especially in terms of the expectations that he or she derives from these experiences. However, it is usually not productive to spend too much time raking over the past. Identity emerges out of teenagers' current experiences, which, ultimately, have more to do with how they see the future than what happened to them in the past. As long as you give your teenager the message that the past does not need to be limiting, it is best to focus on the present and how the future looks from your child's point of view.

Q: How does identity development explain persistent self-destructive or aggressive behavior in teens?

A: Such behaviors may not make sense to someone looking at them from the outside, but they *do* make sense from the point of view of the teen who is acting that way. This is precisely why trying to modify such behaviors through reward and punishment doesn't work. Punishing aggression that seems totally justified to a teenager may make him or her uncomfortable, but it isn't very likely to deter future aggression. To alter persistent aggressive behavior that is the result of an identity based in an adversarial view of the world, you need to alter that worldview.

We all act in response to how we perceive the world, and how we see ourselves, regardless of the potential reward or punishment. People can (and often do) behave in certain ways just to prove that others can't bribe or punish them into behaving differently. The best possibility for changing teenagers' behavior is by understanding who they think they are, and helping them change that negative image.

3

bringing your child
in from the cold
parenting the alienated teen

MORE AND MORE parents today find themselves faced with the challenge of raising a teenage son or daughter who is deeply alienated—from them, from school, from religion, from mainstream society, or all four. Alienation is another identity trap.

Alienated teens dress, talk, and act in ways that challenge authority and communicate cynicism. They may show a disregard for rules, a disdain for school, and disrespect for authority. There are, of course, degrees of alienation, from mild to severe; however, the problem is that once it begins, alienation can quickly escalate because of the consequences it typically reaps. Alienated youths can spiral downward to the point where they find themselves on the outside (of society) looking in.

Reality Check: Ian the Outsider

Ian, the older of two brothers, came from an educated family. They "lived in one of the less expensive houses in a really good neighborhood." Ian's parents were professionals, and both had worked hard to get where they were. They lived a comfortable but by no means extravagant lifestyle. They did believe, though, in the value of quality family time, and they made it a priority to take two family vacations a year. They preferred to take the boys to interesting places as opposed to amusement parks and other common tourist destinations. At thirteen, Ian had already hiked in the rain forests of Costa Rica, swum with porpoises in the Florida Keys, and gone cross-country skiing in Yellowstone National Park, among other similar adventures.

According to Ian's parents, Ian had always had "a mind of his own," sometimes had a hard time conforming to rules, and could, at times, be challenging to adults. In elementary school, for example, he would often question rules—not rebelliously—but to understand why they existed. Some teachers reacted better to this than others, but because they needed to maintain structure and order, none of them showed a great deal of tolerance for it. Later, Ian's questioning moved from rules to ideas, including ideas that struck him as nonsense. One teacher remarked during a conference with Ian's parents that their son could easily be voted "most likely to provoke a controversy."

Through his middle school years Ian was a bit shorter than most of the other boys in his class. He was slight, which made him the target for bullies who made his life miserable, particularly in fifth grade. They threatened him daily on the school bus, jostled him at every opportunity, and stole money and other things from his book bag.

When Ian's father found out about the bullying, he met with school administrators. The bullies were called in, confronted, and warned. They told the school bus driver to be vigilant, and moved Ian to the front of the bus.

These interventions reduced the bullying on the bus, but Ian found that being moved carried a certain stigma. The other kids smiled about it often, which embarrassed him. Worse, still, the bullying didn't really end. The venue merely shifted as the bullies exacted their revenge.

> **HEADS UP!** "Alienation" has two faces—confrontation and creativity. Nurture the positive face.

How to Find and Nurture the Positive Side of an Alienated Teen

Many (though not all) alienated teens show signs early on of being somewhat nonconforming or challenging. Many of these youths are very bright. They often have a capacity to think critically. It's as if they were born with an inner sense that they are individuals, and that they do not have to accept everything they are told. As they look around, they may see or hear something that does not make sense, and rather than simply going along, they question it. If this describes your son or daughter, it's important not to extinguish this individuality, because it is the foundation of what will eventually become your child's identity. Of course, you need to establish and enforce limits, but you must also accept that your child may question you—question all authority. As frustrating as this may be, keep in mind that some of the people who had personalities like this were also responsible for books like *Common Sense* by Thomas Paine and documents like the Declaration of Independence.

Ian's experience of being bullied, and then feeling stigmatized, didn't help his tendency to challenge authority. Despite their efforts, he felt his father and the school administrators had not only failed to protect him, but had actually made matters worse by singling him out. This probably contributed to his feeling like an outsider.

By the time he was twelve Ian had built a reputation for being a difficult student. He would get attention by challenging his teachers, by questioning them, ignoring them, or cursing them in a stage whisper when they turned their backs to him. This helped to alleviate his earlier feelings of weakness and vulnerability, and allowed him to present a tough image. His parents belonged to the community center, and Ian had taken up weight lifting with some good results. He'd gained weight and grown, and no longer made a weak and vulnerable impression. He wore his hair on the long side, liked to wear baggy clothes, and had an affinity for knives. He owned a dozen or more of them, and though he never brought one to school, he always slept with one under his pillow.

Things really went downhill after Ian was arrested for possession of a small amount of marijuana. His parents hired an attorney, who was successful in getting the charge dropped on a technicality. Still, the school took a watchful approach, of which Ian was very aware and to which he responded with hostility. Again, his words reveal his sense of himself: "They look at me like I'm a criminal," he complained with evident disdain for his teachers, unwilling to take any responsibility for the why the school administration might see him as an at-risk youth.

Ian, like most alienated youths, was in the process of building an identity as an outsider, which, in turn, was beginning to determine his behavior. In word and deed, he started acting out the role of an outsider, and became increasingly impervious to the rewards or punishments that either the school or his parents tried to use to influence his behavior and attitudes. Grounding him didn't work. Promises of privileges didn't work. In fact, Ian cursed and criticized teachers more, stopped doing any schoolwork, and started failing all his courses. Threats of summer school or forfeited vacations didn't succeed in motivating him either.

Before long, the school told Ian's parents, they were concerned that Ian might represent a danger to the safety of other students or staff. They were beginning to fear that he might assault, stab, or even shoot someone. In these post-Columbine days, school administrators tend to be on a hair trigger when it comes to identifying and intervening with students they perceive as potential threats, and it's easier than most parents think for a teen to come under suspicion. Even vague, joking threats or taunts that teens are notorious for can lead to a quick suspension.

> **HEADS UP!** *Punishment and criticism won't change your child's outsider identity; in fact, they will only strengthen it.*

Maybe your son or daughter is as alienated as Ian was; or, perhaps, his or her alienation is at an earlier stage. In either case, the thing to remember is that, when it comes to alienation, the situation can deteriorate rapidly. For Ian, his arrest and the increased scrutiny he found himself under led to a downward spiral. For another teen, a similar experience may result in further feelings of rejection—of being on the outside looking in.

In order to prevent this, and to help guide your child away from an identity as an outsider, it is necessary to focus your attention on who your child thinks he or she is rather than on what he or she does. Ian's behavior was provocative and got the attention of school administrators, whose inclination was to try to eliminate it through threats and punishment. This only confirmed Ian's sense of who he was, and made things worse. To help an alienated teen find a way out of this kind of corner, you need to focus on the identity that is responsible for what your teen is doing or saying.

IAN TODAY

By the end of the school year, Ian had fewer and fewer friends and the school was considering placing him in a special education classroom the following school year. His parents and I agreed that the result of this would most likely be to solidify Ian's image of himself as a "road warrior" of the type played by Mel Gibson in the classic film series. Fortunately, Ian's parents had enough resources to place him in a private school, at least for one year. At first, Ian resisted. He didn't want to be sent away, he said, "to a school for delinquents and losers." His parents explained they had carefully researched the school and that it was a private Quaker school, which specialized in serving teens who were truly unique but who didn't fit in at the typical high school—quite the opposite of a dumping ground for problem teens.

Ian relented and agreed to visit the school, after which he said he would try it. By the time he was about to leave for the school, Ian was expressing outright eagerness to go. He acknowledged to me that he didn't "fit in here," and that "the kids I met on my visit there were much more like me than the kids I go to school with here, the teachers were really respectful, not critical, and everyone seemed to get along without a lot of hassles." As Ian described it, each "house" at the school was run by consensus, with the students and resident staff agreeing on house rules that made sense to everyone. Students were as likely as staff to enforce the rules, an arrangement that allowed Ian to see himself in a new light, and in time he began to demonstrate leadership skills instead of his earlier oppositional and defiant behavior.

In Ian's emerging worldview and identity as an outsider, it was him versus everyone else. His interest in weapons, like his interest in building muscle mass, reflected his determination to make himself as invulnerable as possible. It made sense to him, but it was a trap. In meetings with his parents and me prior to leaving for the new school, he talked more and more aggressively about how he didn't care what anyone thought of him, how he didn't need any friends, how his teachers were jerks, and how he would beat up anyone who crossed him. He seemed to take pride in being the consummate outsider and lone survivor in a world gone mad—again, very much like Mel Gibson's Mad Max character.

Although identity is something that emerges from within, and has tremendous motivational power, the experiences teens have can influence the identity they eventually embrace. You could see how Ian's early experiences with bullying and the reaction his teachers had to his challenging personality contributed to his image of himself as someone on the outside looking in. Although those experiences shed some light on his emerging identity, focusing only on those experiences would change nothing—only new experiences, leading to new perceptions of himself, could change the course Ian was headed in. Although the teachers and administrators in his community school were genuinely concerned for his welfare, there seemed to be no viable way for Ian to climb out of the trap he was in if he remained in that school.

Fortunately, he was able to go to the Quaker school, where he was able to benefit from new experiences.

> **HEADS UP!** Learn about what's going on in your child's life, and reinforce an identity based on competence and value.

The Impact of an Experience on Forming Your Child's Identity

Keep your eyes open for experiences that may play a role in influencing your child's emerging identity, particularly experiences that cause her or him to see her- or himself as competent and/or valued by others, as opposed to incompetent or outcast. Point out such experiences as often as you can. Make comments like "That must have made you feel good," "You have a talent for that," and "I'll bet your friends thought that was cool" as often as possible. Regularly ask your child how school is going, and how she or he is enjoying sports, dancing, or any other activities your child enjoys. Ask also about interactions with peers, friends, and teachers, using open-ended questions such as, "Which of your teachers do you like the best? Why?" "Any teachers you don't care for? Why?" "What's the social scene like at school these days?" and "What are you enjoying most about school these days?"

As you engage your teen in this dialogue, try to be alert for experiences that seem to have had an effect, either positively or negatively, on your teen's self-image. You may not like what you hear, or agree with what your teen has to say, but I guarantee that you will be surprised at just how much you can discover about your son or daughter's view of him- or herself and the world by keeping this dialogue going. It will be like seeing the world through your teen's eyes. You can't, of course, control your child's experiences or shield your child from every negative experience, but you can point out the positive and help your teen maintain a more balanced self-image.

■　■　■

One of the most dramatic examples of how even a single experience can help to mold identity and change the course of a teenager's life can be found in *The Autobiography of Malcolm X.* Malcolm recounts a powerful moment when, as an adolescent, his emerging identity (and his future) was altered by a single interaction. He was in high school and doing very well. One day after class, Malcolm recounts the following interaction with his English teacher:

He told me, "Malcolm, you ought to be thinking about a career. Have you been giving it thought?"

I have never figured out why I told him, "Well, yes, sir, I've been thinking I'd like to be a lawyer."

Mr. Ostrowski looked surprised, I remember, and leaned back in his chair and clasped his hands behind his head. He kind of half-smiled and said, "Malcolm, one of life's first needs is for us to be realistic. Don't misunderstand me now. We all here like you, you know that. But you've got to be realistic about being a nigger. A lawyer—that's no realistic goal for a nigger. You need to think about something you *can* be."

The more I thought afterwards about what he said, the more uneasy it made me. It just kept treading around in my mind... It was then that I began to change—inside. I drew away from white people. I came to class, and I answered when called upon. It became a physical strain simply to sit in Mr. Ostrowski's class.

This interaction, which fairly screamed out about limited expectations and closed doors, and coming as it did when Malcolm was a teenager in the process of finding an identity, altered the course of his life. It was an experience he apparently did not share at the time with anyone who could have done something to alter its impact on his emerging view of himself, and it had a devastating effect on his identity.

Shortly after this event, Malcolm left that school and community—and the possibilities they represented—and moved to a city. He also abandoned his vision of becoming an attorney. Instead, he came to place his faith in men like "Jumpsteady," a successful burglar who had an uncanny ability to jump from roof to roof and maneuver along window ledges. He became a numbers runner and then a burglar. Eventually he was caught and went to prison, where he went by the intimidating moniker *Satan*.

> **HEADS UP!** *Remember the people who made a difference for you.*

Imagine how things might have turned out if, on that fateful afternoon, Mr. Ostrowski had opened the doors of possibility instead of closing them. What if he'd said, "That's a great plan, Malcolm!"? How might things have turned out if Malcolm had shared this experience with someone who saw its implications for his identity, and responded in a way that would have allowed Malcolm to see it as only one of many alternative directions his life could take? Almost everyone I talk to can name one or two adults who had an impact on their lives, sometimes all it took was a single interaction. One professional athlete told me of a high school coach who, after watching him play tag football, came up to him and said, "Why don't you try out for the football team? I think you'd be a good addition." That proved to be as life altering an interaction—in a positive way—as Malcolm's interaction with his teacher was in a negative way.

Thinking back on your own life, can you recall one or two specific experiences that influenced your sense of who you were and what possibilities the future might hold for you? How did these experiences affect you?

INDIVIDUALS: OUTSIDERS WITH POSITIVE IDENTITIES

One way to rescue teens like Ian, who are drifting toward alienation and an identity trap, is to expose them to experiences that have the potential to help them see themselves in a different light. Such kids tend to see themselves as outsiders, which generates shame and resentment and leads to a defiant stance, which is a recipe for disaster. Alienation contributes to drug abuse, violence, and self-destructiveness. Many teens who cut themselves see themselves as outsiders, as do most violent, truant, and drug-abusing teens. Regardless of how popular they may be, or how others may see them, privately they feel as if they do not fit in. To understand self-destructive behavior, parents need to understand its roots in this outsider identity.

An alternative, postive, and no less legitimate way of being an outsider is to see yourself as a true individual. Being an *individual* is a much more self-respectful identity, one that can lead to feelings of pride rather than shame or anger. Whereas outsiders quickly become used to being seen as defective and inferior (and to privately thinking of themselves that way, as well), being an individual means being "different" but not inferior.

Though they rarely admit it, outsiders do feel inferior and defective. They are keenly aware of—and even exaggerate—any perceived flaws. Ian, for instance, did not feel that he was intelligent or attractive, despite clear evidence, such as early report cards and photos, to the contrary. Adolescent girls who think of themselves as outsiders harbor similar feelings. In fact, since research suggests that girls today may be even more competitive with each other than most boys are, teenage girls tend to exaggerate their perceived limitations and flaws even more.

Moving toward an identity as an outsider can be a vicious cycle; that is, adolescents who start out unique and different behave in some way that provokes a response. They may be as challenging and outspoken as Ian was, and, like him, they may want to present themselves as tough. Alternatively, they may present themselves as extremely weak and vulnerable by cutting themselves, for example, or expressing suicidal ideas. Some outsiders become criminals; others may find themselves repeatedly admitted to psychiatric hospitals; and still others fall victim to addiction.

HEADS UP! Don't live in the past.

Although alienation has its causes, you should avoid endless discussions of them with your teenage son or daughter. Such discussions usually are counterproductive in that they can lead your child to feeling even more depressed or angry than he or she already is. Teens' eyes invariably glaze over when parents (or therapists!) insist on analyzing the past. Understanding the past may be more important to you than it is to your son or daughter, who is living in the present and is rightly more concerned with tomorrow than with yesterday.

Just as being aware of your child's day-to-day experiences and how your teen views the world can provide you with clues to the identity your child may be moving toward, so can reflecting on your child's past. At the same time, because the past can't be undone, and because teens are usually loath to dwell on it, it's more productive to keep your discussions focused on today and tomorrow rather than yesterday or years ago. Resist any urge you may have to rake over the past. Simply talking about Ian's experiences of being bullied was not likely to lead to a change in his identity. What he needed was experiences that would allow him to see himself as a capable young man with a bright future.

Guiding Your Teen . . . Away from Alienation

There are specific things that parents can do that can help steer a teen away from an emerging identity as an alienated "outsider" to someone who is an "individual" not cut from the same mold as everyone else. Keep in kind that whereas "outsiders" are prone to feeling anger and resentment, "individuals" can be justly proud of the personal qualities that set them apart from others.

THREE GUIDELINES TO HELP YOUR TEEN MOVE FROM OUTSIDER TO INDIVIDUAL

Guideline #1: Acknowledge it. Instead of trying to talk a teen out of being an outsider, begin by acknowledging that this is the identity that he or she seems to be moving toward. Getting your child to accept this idea is crucial to moving her or him away from it. With Ian, I simply said, "It seems like you're starting to see yourself as something of an outsider." You can do the same with your teen. However, try not to say it in a challenging or critical way, which is likely to get a defensive denial than an honest acknowledgement.

Guideline #2: Try substituting the word "individual" for the word "outsider." When I suggested that Ian had always been something of an individual, not someone inclined to go along with the crowd, he and his parents heartily nodded. Nobody in the room minded the idea that Ian was an individual. This provided a clear opening for Ian to begin thinking of himself not as an alienated outsider, but as a unique individual; someone who didn't fit the mold of a typical teen, but who was by no means inferior or defective. In time that was exactly the direction toward which his identity moved.

Naturally, for Ian's identity to shift in that direction, he had to believe this was true. My saying it was no guarantee that he would embrace this idea. He needed to have some evidence to support this perception, which, fortunately, his parents were able to provide by giving him a fresh start. It was all too clear—to me, to Ian, and to his parents—that somewhere along the line, others stopped seeing his behavior as a sign of an individualistic, nonconformist personality, and had begun to see it as a sign of an antisocial personality in the works. Worse still, Ian had begun to embrace this identity and was quickly becoming an angry, antisocial young man, moving rapidly toward seeing himself as "the baddest dude on the block," and to viewing the world as a fundamentally hostile place.

If your teen's identity is moving toward alienation, try to remember if your child exhibited signs of individualism from an early age.

These signs can provide evidence of an alternative identity: as an individual rather than an outcast. Then, do the following:

- Share your observations with your son or daughter.

- Suggest that these qualities are the signs of someone who is not run-of-the-mill, not ordinary, but rather of someone with a mind of his or her own, who occupies a unique place in the world.

Guideline 3: Celebrate nonconformity. Your teen will most likely not embrace an identity as an individual if you yourself are uncomfortable with it. To help make that a viable identity you have to communicate respect for it. This may take a bit of honest soul-searching on your part, but imagine how Ian might have responded if his parents pointed out that he was always unique, even challenging, and that *they disapproved of that.* Clearly, that would only have reinforced his identity as an alienated youth.

Adolescence is that time in our lives when we simultaneously struggle with two competing needs: the need to be accepted and to fit in, and the need to be an individual and stand out. As you reflect on what your teenager is going through and struggle to make sense of his or her actions and attitudes, keep this inner conflict in mind. Let your teen know that you know what he or she is struggling with. Point out ways in which your child is an individual and unique, as well as ways in which they fit in and are accepted by their peers.

FAQs

Q: Is there a way to prevent adolescent alienation?
A: I believe it may indeed be possible to prevent alienation by maintaining a very cohesive family life. However, doing so might mean

that you must make significant lifestyle changes and sacrifices. The need for both parents to work to support a family plus the prevalence of single-parent and blended families are impediments to the kind of tightly knit family life that might keep a child from being exposed to alienating ideas and other alienated teens. In addition, preventing alienation would mean being willing and able to extensively supervise and censor what a teen is exposed to. This is not feasible for most parents today, although there are some actions you can take to help make your family more cohesive and thereby minimize the chances for alienation to set in.

Q: How does alienation get started?

A: There is no one common pathway to alienation that all teens follow, although there are some risk factors for alienation. Among them are academic failure and social rejection, difficulty being recognized and accepted as an individual, and drug abuse. Also, certain personality traits and temperaments, such as hyperactivity and emotional sensitivity, may be risk factors for alienation. As a rule society seems to be most accepting of behaviors, beliefs, and temperaments which fall within what we might call "the middle of the bell curve." Conversely, the farther a child deviates from this middle range, in terms of attitudes, temperaments, or behaviors, the more at risk he or she becomes for interventions aimed at moving them toward the middle of the spectrum of acceptable behavior. Once a teen begins to see her- or himself as someone who is on the outside, there are a multitude of ways that this emerging identity can be reinforced, including the lyrics to music, movies, and fads in clothing. The best you can do is be vigilant; be on the lookout for any of these risk factors, and, if you see one, do what you can to reduce it as soon as possible. You can also help your child to view diversity—in him- or herself as well as in others—as a sign of individuality rather than inferiority.

Q: My teenage daughter finds fault in everything I do or say. How do I support her individuality when she keeps pushing me away?

A: The first rule is to avoid constant arguments. Choose your battles carefully. If you feel compelled to respond to a criticism, keep your response brief and avoid attacking. For example, if your teenager expresses an opinion you consider outrageous, just state your own opinion and leave it at that. Don't accuse your child of being outrageous, because that will only play into alienation. Every teen does or says things that parents are bound to object to—indeed, teenagers almost seem compelled to be outrageous at times—but they also say and do plenty of things parents can agree with, praise, or support. Don't be blinded to these things by getting caught up in the things you object to.

Q: How does celebrating nonconformity differ from promoting alienation?

A: There is plenty to praise about nonconformity, which isn't at all the same as alienation. Alienation always includes an element of anger and cynicism; nonconformity, in contrast, can be creative and friendly. Adolescence is a time for testing limits, but it is also a time for creativity. When you see your teenager doing something that's nonconforming, try thinking of it as something creative, rather than combative. See if you can detect joy and excitement, as opposed to anger and cynicism, beneath the words and actions. If you do, then you can celebrate it.

4

the transparent parent
learning about your teen by letting your teen know you

BEING A TRANSPARENT parent means providing your son or daughter with a window into your own thinking, your priorities, why you make the decisions you do, and the experiences that helped shape your own identity. Knowing who you are—your goals, your values—can be enormously helpful to your teenager as he or she struggles to form his or her identity. For some reason, many parents choose to remain more or less opaque to their children. They make decisions, select goals, and set priorities, but without ever letting their children in on this process. They most certainly do have an identity—a sense of who they are and why they are here, what they stand for and what their dreams are—but they never talk about these things, or reveal any of the formative experiences that shaped their identity. They are, in a word, closed books. Often, they had parents who were also closed books. Typically, they express the belief that their children would not be interested in these things, which is rarely true. Can you remember being interested in knowing more about your own parents? Did you find this topic boring? Chances are you were very interested in knowing more about what your parents thought, and how they came to be the people they were.

How reasonable is it to expect children to learn to make good decisions or choose healthy identities if their parents are opaque about their own decisions and formative experiences? I am not suggesting that you begin a continuous monologue about every thought you have or every decision you make. Nor am I suggesting that you recount your entire autobiography to your teenage son or daughter. That's generally more information than your son or daughter wants to know or needs to know! At the same time, I have found that transparency begets transparency, and that, in turn, allows you to have more influence on your child than you will if all you do is give advice or question your child's decisions. In addition, this process becomes a two-way street, one in which your son or daughter begins to be more open to you.

> **HEADS UP!** *Talk about yourself.*

Ways to Communicate Who You Are to Your Teenager

Strive to become more open about how you make decisions, especially important ones. If you are not already, consider being more revealing about such things as:

- How you came to choose your career.

- What you like about your work.

- Decisions you're glad you made, and why.

- Decisions you regret you made, and why.

- How you set priorities—what's most (and least) important to you.

- How you decide whether or not to make a significant purchase.

- What your goals are.

- Why you like your friends.

- People you admire, and why.

- People you do not respect, and why.

- What you look forward to.

- The things that give you the most joy.

YOUR FORMATIVE EXPERIENCES

Since finding an identity is the main psychological business of adolescence, it is natural that a teen's personal experiences weigh heavily in moving him or her toward one identity or another. Abuse and neglect, for example, are powerful experiences that can lead to dysfunctional identities, where victims view themselves as worthless or even bad people. Yet as powerful as they are, even abuse or neglect are not the final determiners of identity. If that were the case then every abused person would have a dysfunctional identity, and we know that is not true. Some victims of abuse do form "dark" identities, but others go on to lead productive, happy, and even inspired lives.

The identity we finally choose crystallizes only when we have one or more crucial experiences that affect us on an emotional level. These *formative* experiences—when they are positive—explain why some victims of abuse don't cave in, but instead choose a healthy identity. Part of adolescence is a search for ideas and people to believe in—for ideals and for heroes—and for experimentation (including experimenting with who you can be), and all of these are factors that influence the identity your teenager will ultimately embrace.

Reality Check: Kate the Winner (and Mom) vs. Amy the Goth (and Daughter)

One day in gym class during Kate's junior year, all the girls were required to run a timed fifty-yard dash. She had never done this before, and was anxious and self-conscious. All she could picture was being the last one across the finish line, and everyone laughing at her. As it turned out, Kate ran the dash and achieved the second best time of all the junior girls. The best time was run by a classmate, she barely knew, named Sara. Sara was on the track team; Kate wasn't. Later that day when Kate was having ice cream at a local hangout when Sara came up to her and said, "I heard about your time today. Nice going, girl!" They had never spoken to each other before that, but their friendship began right there. Kate had never thought of herself as anything other than an average athlete, but from that day forward she thought of herself as just as a fast and agile athlete, which affected her view of herself and, more important perhaps, it affected the way she played sports and her interest in them. In college, Kate made varsity in soccer and was on a team that won an NCAA title. According to Kate, from that day on, she thought of herself as a winner.

Early in Kate's senior year, she was selected to give a short speech at an assembly of the entire student body. She was petrified at the prospect; dreading it for days. On the day of the speech, looking out at the sea of faces. she says she had no notion what she talked about or for how long she talked, but she does remember that while she was up there, she had two distinct thoughts. One was the realization that, against all odds, she was actually going to get through it and was probably going to survive the experience. The other was the amazement that all these other kids were quietly listening to her. Holding the audience in the palm of her hand like that was powerful experience, and, Kate put it, "I walked out on the stage as a scared, skinny seventeen-year-old; but I walked off it as a leader of my class and of the school."

That same senior year, Kate's high school did its usual food-baskets-for-the-poor project. She was part of a small group that delivered the bounty to one family the last day of school before Christmas vacation. The family lived in a neighborhood she had never seen before. It was winter, and the house was missing its front door, a blanket hung where the door should have been. Kate vividly remembers that there was a guy zonked out on the couch who never stirred while the group was in the house, and that there was a harried, tired-looking woman and five or six little kids running around. The students piled up all the food baskets and the wrapped presents. The kids were quite excited and the woman gave them a wan little smile and said thank you, and that was that. Even then Kate realized that this do-gooder activity by a group of high school kids probably did not much change that family, but to Kate, it was the first "important" thing she had ever done. This was not what kids did. This was what adults did.

That Kate could recall these three experiences so vividly nearly twenty years later demonstrates just how formative they were. It is also attested to by the fact that Kate went on to become a social worker, and, because of her organizational and interpersonal skills, she was now an associate director of a large agency that served families and children. She and her husband, John, struggled to maintain a middle-class life and raise two daughters, the younger of whom had just turned fourteen. Maintaining this lifestyle required two full-time jobs, which meant that family life was squeezed into weekends and evenings.

Kate was worried about her younger daughter, Amy. Her older daughter, Julie, was a freshman in college, and though she had had some issues—including a brief flirtation with anorexia at age fifteen—she was doing okay.

Amy, on the other hand, had turned, seemingly overnight, "from a princess into a vampire," Kate told me. A girl who a year before would not be caught in anything but preppy clothing, and who loved short skirts that showed off her shapely legs, was now a study in oversize black: black baggy pants, black baggy tops, black baggy coat. Her makeup matched her clothes: black eyeliner, black mascara; even black lip outliner. She'd recently cut her hair (by herself) very short and dyed it jet black, and the tasteful silver jewelry she once preferred was steadily being replaced by clunky chains and leather bracelets. She and Kate were in a daily battle over how many body piercings Amy could have. Kate wanted to limit her to two in each ear, four in all. Amy insisted that she be allowed to pierce herself anywhere she wanted, including her navel, eyebrow, and maybe even her tongue. Kate suspected that the next battle would be over tattoos.

Why had Amy turned "goth"? Was this a dangerous sign? Was Kate right to be worried? Teenagers always have flirted (and always will experiment) with different identities before they settle on one. These identities are indeed like different sets of clothes; each is associated with different activities, different friends, and different music. Contrary to Kate's fears, a goth look is not necessarily a sign of impending doom. It does not necessarily imply that your child is heavily involved with drugs or sex, satanic beliefs, or even angry and alienated. However, when a teen turns goth *and* begins to show an interest in satanic notions *and* falls into a steep decline academically *and* starts hanging out with known drug users, *then* you need to be concerned.

Amy was not there yet   not even close.

Reality Check: Satanic Scott

In contrast to Amy, sixteen-year-old Scott, who had been living the good life in a California suburb, was transformed in the span of two years from a clean-cut kid with cropped sandy hair who wore jeans and T-shirts to a goth with dyed black shoulder-length hair and an all-black wardrobe, who isolated himself from all of his old friends and read a satanic bible over lunch in the school cafeteria. Not long after his transformation, Scott was charged with murdering a neighbor. The motive? He believed the neighbor might have run over and killed his dog.

It's easy, and perhaps tempting, to write off a tragedy like this to mental illness—the act of a deranged mind. As a parent, though, you can't afford the luxury of such simple answers. The more likely explanation was that Scott was in the process of embracing a dark identity—an angry outsider, who would take revenge against those he thought would injure him, and, unfortunately, this dark identity allowed him to do what he did. His actions made sense to him in the context of who he thought he was, which, in a way, is even scarier that the idea that he was just a deranged kid, which actually is a rare exception.

The reasons for Scott's embrace of this dark identity may have had to do with the fact that his family was in the process of disintegrating, and, as a result, there appeared to be a progressive loss of any meaningful connection between him and his parents. In place of a parent–child bond stood a wall of angry alienation. Under these circumstances, a teenager, like Scott, does not see—indeed, doesn't want to see—who his parents are or what they stand for. Parents who allow this wall to stand do so at their (and their child's) peril.

What to do When Your Teen Flirts with the Goth Side

Naturally, you should monitor your teenager if you see him or her adopting a goth look, but you need to look deeper than external appearance. Many teens who become drug addicts or who end up on the wrong side of the law, look quite normal. It's what's going on *inside* your child that counts. You need to assess your teen's attitudes about adults as well as about society as a whole. Maintaining transparent, two-way communication is the best way to prevent what happened with Scott from happening with your teenager. It will help you determine whether the things your child says and does reveal a growing hostility toward the world. For example, does your teenager seem to feel that the world is against him or her? Does your child express cynicism about your own values and priorities, espouse a belief in the devil, or show disdain for all adults? If that is the case, he or she may be moving toward a dark identity. In the absence of these other signals, though, it is possible your teen is merely flirting with a different look, albeit one that arouses concern. This is especially likely if, because of your transparent relationship with your teen, it is clear to you that your child does not reject your core values.

Open communication will always give you vital insights into what's going on inside your child and whether it is something to be concerned about. Questions to keep in mind include:

- *Is there a formative experience or experiences that seem to be related to any negative changes you are seeing?* For example, did it follow on the heels of a divorce, or problems with bullying? In Scott's case, it did. His sister was killed in an accident two years earlier, following which his parents became embroiled in and preoccupied with a long and nasty divorce. Clearly, in this context of family disintegration, the future must have seemed quite dismal to Scott, who appears to have gotten lost as his world fell apart around him. It is not difficult (although it certainly may be frightening) to see how a youth like Scott might turn toward Satan as his hero.

  In contrast, Amy readily admitted to her mother that her transformation was driven primarily by a desire to try on a different look. She'd grown tired of the preppy look, and also the competitive nature of that teenage subculture. Goths, she explained, were less competitive with each other, and less obsessed with their social status. Because Amy's "gothic period" was not the result of desperation, and did not reflect any deep alienation from her mother's values, it would most likely disappear in the same way it came, and not become her final identity. In Amy's case, it was a *transitional identity:* something between her preppy stage and the individual she would eventually become.

- *Have there been any changes in school performance or attendance associated with a change in your teen's appearance or attitudes?* The differences between Scott and Amy were striking. She continued to do as well in school as she had during her preppy days; Scott, in contrast, took a steep academic nosedive.

- *Are there signs of alienation from your own core values and priorities?* Amy may have argued with her mother—but since when is that news in any teenage daughter–mother relationship? The bottom line is that Amy remained engaged with her mother. She did not drift away or become alienated. In words and deeds, she continued to show that she was fundamentally a kind and caring person. She did not ignore holidays or birthdays. She remained on friendly terms with her old preppy friends while building new friendships among the more laid-back goths. And so on. There were no signs of the anger or cynicism that is the hallmark of true alienation. These signs were very evident, however, in Scott's case, He began using drugs regularly, and he became an avid Satanist and social isolate.

When Kate asked herself these questions, she concluded that she did not have to worry about Amy. She knew she needed to continue to set limits (body piercings, tattoos, etc.), but she no longer felt the panic that had been keeping her awake at night. At one point, when things between her and Amy were particularly good, she remarked that she understood that Amy was experimenting with different looks partly as a way of discovering who she wanted to be, and even confided that she never much cared for the preppy culture herself!

Fight as they might, communication between Kate and Amy remained open. They were fairly transparent to one another, and bonded to one other. As a consequence, Amy's struggle to find an identity was marked by more good times than bad ones. Mother and daughter could argue one minute, then share a laugh the next. That was hardly true for Scott.

Reality Check: Mad Martin

Having just turned twenty-one a few weeks earlier, Martin spent a night in jail after getting into an altercation with another young man who he thought was being rude to his girl-friend. It was Martin's first arrest, and his first exposure to jail, but not his first brush with trouble because of his temper. When he came to see me as a condition of his probation, Martin's formative experiences had led him toward a dark and problematic identity, but, fortunately, an identity that had not yet completely hardened.

In his senior year in high school, Martin attended anger management classes after getting into a series of scuffles that culminated in a five-day suspension. Since he had a job and no prior record, the judge had approved Martin's release contingent on his getting counseling for anger management. He attended the classes and got a certificate of completion, which the court accepted, but he hadn't really changed.

Martin had a girlfriend he described as "a sweetheart," affectionate and accommodating. Still, at times he found himself losing his temper even with her. When I asked Martin if he had always been prone to blowing up, he said no. On the contrary, as a child he'd been rather sensitive and had a strong negative reaction to other people's anger. He recalled liking to draw and read, and didn't mind spending time alone doing these things. He also remembered being teased because he was not particularly good at competitive sports. "I didn't like fighting, either, and I would always look for a way to avoid a confrontation. That didn't earn me a lot of points with my peers."

I asked Martin to begin a journal, and, in particular, to think and write about experiences that had a strong emotional impact on him as well as recollections of who his heroes were—either real or fictional—when he was growing up.

One entry simply read, "Rambo." Later, he explained that from about age eight to twelve he'd been fascinated by Sylvester Stallone's portrayal of an ex-military man who becomes a virtual one-man army, fighting the enemies of America and avenging their victims. Martin's father had been a Marine who left when he was barely three years old. Martin's sole memory of his father was of a tall, sturdy man in uniform, standing in his doorway looking at him as he lay in bed, then turning and walking away.

As much as he loved watching Rambo movies, Martin said that he never thought of himself in that way, at least not then. He admired Rambo for his courage, but he never imagined being Rambo; nor did he playact the role. Recently, however, Rambo and what he stood for had assumed great meaning and significance for him—something to believe in.

When Martin was sixteen years old, he was a six-foot, strapping youth, although he still preferred compromise to confrontation, and had little interest in competitive sports. He, his mother, and his younger sister lived in a modest home in a decent neighborhood that abutted one that was considerably less desirable. A significant number of kids from this other, tougher neighborhood attended the same schools as Martin and his sister, and there were the inevitable "culture" clashes and incursions.

One day Martin arrived home from school and found his mother and sister in the kitchen. His mother was applying a cold compress to the side of his sister's head. Her eyes were swollen and bloodshot from crying, and she had a red welt on that side of her face from an altercation with three girls on the school grounds. Martin recalled feeling very depressed for several days after this incident.

The second experience came barely a month later. Martin was returning home from school, and spotted a boy fooling around with his sister's bike, which was chained to a fence. As he approached, he realized the boy was trying to cut through the chain with a bolt cutter. In Martin's words, something within him "snapped" when he realized what was happening. "I didn't think, I just moved," he said. "I heard myself yelling, and then I charged. I can still that kid's eyes when he saw me coming. He didn't have time to move. I barreled into him, knocked him down, and started pummeling him. I hit him a bunch of times before he managed to squirm loose and run."

Martin vividly recalled the feeling of exhilaration that followed on the heels of this experience. "It felt incredibly good," he said, "to see that kid running away from me like that." I kept running the scene through my mind for weeks.

Martin linked these two experiences with his current tough-guy identity. Though he had not thought about Rambo, he had long prided himself on being a tough guy, who would not tolerate abuse or disrespect, and would not back down from a confrontation. He was keenly sensitive to being disrespected, and could see how that attitude extended to the way he treated his girlfriend and had led to the latest altercation. At the same time, Martin admitted that inwardly he tended to be insecure and prone to periodic bouts of depression and anxiety. He worried about the future, and described himself as someone who went through life "watching his back."

Once he became aware of how his identity had formed, and how his behavior since age sixteen had largely been a reflection of that identity, Martin realized that he had actually made a choice: to be tough. This, in turn, meant that he could make other choices, even now: He could continue to be a tough guy or he could carve out a new identity, one based in different experiences and ideals. It became clear to him that if he identified himself as a tough guy, no amount of "anger management training" would make a difference. It wasn't his lack of anger management skills that accounted for the hair-trigger temper; rather, it was his view of the world as a hostile place and his need to see himself as someone who demanded respect and would not be victimized that drove his actions.

Martin spent a good deal of time revisiting his early memories of himself as a sensitive, artistic individual—in effect, who he was as a child. He also allowed himself to experience the sadness of not having a father to look after him, and, equally important, of not having a real father on whom he could model himself. Instead, he chose a fictional character that was close to that single image he had of his father. If his father hadn't left, Martin could have developed a more transparent, three-dimensional picture of his father, and his own identity might have taken a different direction. He was amazed that so much of his identity hinged on that single memory of his father and those two formative experiences with his sister. He decided to see if he could "let go of Rambo" long enough to open himself to other experiences that might offer the possibility of a different identity and a new path to follow.

The case of Martin also illustrates that while it's important not to focus exclusively on the past, understanding how past experiences may have influenced identity development can be valuable. Again, my point is not that the past is irrelevant, only that it does hold the cure. Once a parent has a clue as to what kind of identity is forming in a teen, and what influenced it, the challenge then becomes to focus on new experiences in the here and now, and on the concept of choice. Martin's identity began to change only when he realized he had a choice for the future, and chose to pursue that choice.

The Impact of Emotional Experience on Your Teenager's Identity

In some respects, the process by which each of us forms an identity in our teenage years is simple: We look for people and ideas to believe in, and we look around to see what alternative paths are open to us. Both Amy and Martin were doing that, as Kate had done in her youth. Ultimately, however, your child's identity crystallizes with the help of one or more emotionally significant experiences. Your child may even choose an identity knowing you and others will disapprove of, or which seems at variance with who he or she once was, if it fills some greater need, as for example Martin's need for self-respect.

Knowing this, you can see how forming an identity can be fraught with dangers, and how it can be subject to many influences that can lead your teenager to choose a dark identity over a radiant one. The challenge is to do all you can to promote healthy ideals and values, to help your child see as many positive alternatives as possible, to believe without fail in his or her potential, and to shield him or her as best you can from the kinds of formative experiences that might lead toward a dark identity.

AMY, SCOTT, AND MARTIN TODAY

By striving to be more transparent, especially about the important things in your life, you can offer your child valuable food for thought as your son or daughter makes his or her journey toward identity. That's what Kate did for Amy. She shared with her daughter the three formative experiences she'd experienced as well as other ones. Rather than just asking Amy questions, she began to share some of her own thoughts and feelings about certain decisions she needed to make about her job, friendships, and family.

Amy is now a senior in high school, and still doing well academically. Her looks have evolved along with her identity. She works part-time in a local food market. Her preferred wardrobe lies somewhere between gothic and chic. She is a true individual—not one of the crowd. She volunteers one Saturday a month at a local nursing home, where she plays board games and organizes book discussions for the residents, who look forward to her visits. She still dyes her hair black, and prefers it short, and she has a tattoo of a rose on her ankle. After graduation, she plans to go to nursing school, and thinks that she might want to specialize in pediatric nursing. Like her mother, Amy is more concerned with the quality of her relationships than with her social status.

Scott, unfortunately, remains the victim of his dark identity, and likely faces a long prison sentence. On the other hand, Martin has successfully moved beyond his Rambo identity. He now sees himself as a fundamentally sensitive individual, one who can be "tough" if need be, but who does not need to see himself as a stranger in a strange land. He has allowed himself to pursue some of the interests he let go of as he morphed into Rambo. One of his dearest wishes now is to be able to father a child some day and to be there as that child grows. He says that he intends to allow his child to see who he is, what his goals are, and what he values most in others.

Two Guidelines for Healthy Transparency

Here are some guidelines for how to introduce some healthy transparency into your relationship with your teen. It's important to choose the right time for these kinds of interactions. The best time is when things are going well, you and your teen and not bin conflict, and there is time to talk.

Guideline #1: Share your own formative experiences. As long as they do not feel that they are being lectured to, teenagers usually are interested in hearing about their parents' own adolescence. I encourage parents to share those experiences that stand out in their mind, beginning with the most positive ones but also in time including negative ones, that helped shape their sense of who they were and where their lives were heading. Sharing negative experiences—and how you dealt with them—can encourage your teen to be more open with you. Sharing positive formative experiences communicates optimism— the idea that negative experiences can be overcome.

Guideline #2: Emphasize choice. Always communicate that you understand that your teen is immersed in discovering who she or he is, what she or he stands for, and so on. At the same time, always communicate the idea that he or she is a "work in progress", not in a negative sense but in the sense that there are choices that can be made, and different directions that can be pursued.

FAQs

Q: Is it okay for me to share my doubts and anxieties about decisions with my teenager?

A: Yes, but only if you balance these with positive feelings about decisions you make. If you present yourself as a poster child for indecision and insecurity, don't be surprised if your teenager either turns a deaf ear or models you. If you do suffer from such chronic insecurity, you can do both yourself and your child a favor by seeking counseling to overcome it.

Q: Can I share so-called "negative" experiences from my own past, or do they all have to be positive, uplifting ones?

A: Negative experiences that teach your child a lesson or change her or his priorities, and which in some way can have a positive impact on your teen's identity, can be very useful. For example, one father told his son, who was having some problems with weight, about how he'd been bullied at the start of high school, in part because he was overweight and out of shape. He began a regimen of regular exercise and weightlifting, and within a relatively short period looked so much different that no one ever bothered him again. Moreover, his new look changed his sense of himself, from someone who was inferior, with low expectations, to someone for whom the future held many opportunities.

Q: Are there things about myself that I should not be transparent about?

A: Definitely, beginning with those experiences the sharing of which would serve no good purpose. This is partly a matter of timing. For example, consider experiences that embarrassed you. Just sharing such experiences for the sake of sharing them would seem to serve little purpose. On the other hand, if you discover that your teenager recently had an embarrassing experience, and you can relate to this by sharing a similar experience and how you dealt with it, it can be very therapeutic and can go a long way toward mitigating any potential long-term negative effect the experience might have on your teen. Don't be surprised, though, if you experience a wave of embarrassment when recalling such experiences. Feeling humiliated is not easy to get over, and it can take years before you or your teenager are able to laugh about it.

Q: Are there experiences I should definitely share?

A: Those experiences that stand out in your mind, even today, that affected how you felt about yourself and your future. Sharing experiences that lowered your expectations for the future is okay, *if* they are balanced with experiences that opened possibilities for you and positively affected your view of yourself.

5

parenting a combative teenager
how to establish and maintain
a productive dialogue

CLEARLY, I AM an advocate of open communication between parents and their teenage children, but the kind of communication I favor is not judgmental or advice-oriented; rather, I favor communication that encourages teens to talk more and in doing so to reveal the way they see themselves and their place in the world. This approach allows you to gain valuable insight into the identity that is developing within your teenager. You must still impose certain limits on your child, and communicate your expectations, but if this is done effectively earlier on, beginning at roughly age three, it becomes less critical during adolescence. Still, it is not really possible to avoid all conflict with teens, so don't think your family is abnormal or "dysfunctional" if you find yourself in the position of being the family "cop" at times. That will still leave plenty of opportunities for the kind of communication that will give you a window onto your teen's developing identity.

The Battle of the Parent and the Teen

If you had a typical adolescence, you probably remember one or both of your parents questioning your actions and/or your decisions. Maybe this happened often, or maybe only occasionally. How did you react to it? If you didn't mind being questioned, chances are that your parents questioned you responsibly, and that you realized that they were right to do so, even if you didn't want to admit it. On the other hand, if you resented the questioning, closed down, or even blew up whenever it came to having a dialogue with your parents, chances are that your parents either asked the wrong questions or asked the right questions in the wrong way.

> **HEADS UP!** *Never forget, teenagers love to argue.*

Teenagers love to argue—so much so that I've come to think of this as an innate part of their development, just as infants gurgle and toddlers invent playmates. Teens like to question adults about their values, and they like to test limits. This does not necessarily mean that they do not respect the adults they question, or that they reject their values. On the contrary, I think it is a sign of a healthy parent–teen relationship that this questioning takes place. In an unhealthy relationship, the teen simply becomes alienated from the parent. There is no arguing, no testing, and no real communication of any kind.

Teenagers love to argue. Why? First, they get a sense of themselves as independently functioning human beings. By arguing, they show that they are no longer children. Second, they use their argumentativeness to work out their own values and their identity. In this way, the values and identity they eventually settle on feel like *theirs*, not someone else's. When parents describe their relationships with their teenage children as contentious, I'm inclined to smile and think that all's well in the world; it's when there is no communication that I worry.

> **HEADS UP!** *In the history of the world, no parent has ever won an argument with a teenager.*

The writer F. Scott Fitzgerald once wrote that the sign of a first-rate mind was the ability to hold two opposing ideas simultaneously. The example he used was to know that a situation is hopeless, yet be determined to make it otherwise. You face a similar challenge: to recognize that your teen needs to argue with you, while accepting the fact that you will never win the argument. The best you can hope for is to agree to disagree, with no hard feelings. If you can manage this, I can pretty much guarantee that your teen will turn out okay.

Reality Check: Hothouse Hannah

Hannah, at eight, was a beautiful, bright, and creative child, inquisitive and friendly. She attended a Montessori school, which she liked a great deal and where she was doing very well. Her favorite subjects were math and science; she also loved horses and took riding lessons. When she grew up, she said, she wanted to raise horses or teach.

Hannah's father was an attorney, her mother a librarian. They had an older son, Jed, who as a teenager had given them a run for their money. Jed turned out okay, despite having had one brush with the law and having dropped out of the private college his parents initially insisted he attend. He chose a two-year degree program at a local community college, which he paid for himself; he found a job and worked his way up to a position as an assistant manager in a large sporting goods store. He had his own apartment, a girlfriend, and paid his bills. Although he did not meet his parents' expectations, he had developed a healthy identity and his life was going well.

Hannah's parents assumed that she would not take after her brother, academically or in any other way. On some level, they thought that she would be their reward for all they'd gone through with Jed. They were wrong. Now sixteen, Hannah was a sophomore at a prestigious (and expensive) private high school, but Hannah's academic record was erratic at best. She had a reputation for being smart, but unmotivated, noncon-forming, and a bit rebellious.

Hannah lived in a hypercompetitive world, not just academ-ically but socially. What you wore, where you went on vaca-tion, and who your friends were, was as important as the grades you got. Hannah's parents knew that the school was competi-tive, but they had little idea of just how competitive it was.

By the time she finished her freshman year Hannah had given up trying to compete academically with the "geniuses" in her classes, although she was clearly bright. In addition, although she was a talented pianist who had performed in numerous recitals, she had lost much of her enthusiasm for it · and, to her parents' chagrin, had opted out of several recent competitions. At the same time, she developed a reputation for being the most avant-garde member of her class when it came to hairstyle, jewelry, and clothing. She also wrote satir-ical pieces about faculty, the school, and her peers for the school's monthly newspaper, several of which had nearly been censored, or unceremoniously dropped, by the faculty advisor, who made no secret of her displeasure to Hannah.

It is perhaps understandable that Hannah was driving her parents to distraction. They had never been subtle about their expectations; on the contrary, they were inclined to hover over her. They did more than set limits for her; they tried to impose their will on her. They asked her every day about her studies, wanted to read (and even offered to edit) her reports, and constantly prodded her to do better. They'd press her to go to the library, buy her audio books (which stayed on her night table, unopened), grill her about her assignments, and groan loudly over her progress reports. In their minds, they simply wanted Hannah to be the best person she could be.

HEADS UP! *Never forget, it's your child's life, not yours*

How to Manage Your Expectations and Offer Encouragement

We all want our children to realize their potential. Like the valedictorian at every high school graduation, we can encourage our sons and daughters to set their sights high. There is a difference, however, between encouraging your child not to underestimate him- or herself (and thus to fear setting high goals) and trying to chart the course of your teen's life, which was what Hannah's parents were doing. Consider how you would have responded if someone had told you what your goals should be. The difference between that and just plain encouragement and support is obvious.

It is reasonable and normal for you to have expectations for your children. All caring parents hope that their child will have an easier, better, and more satisfying life. Problems arise when you allow your personal expectations to become your child's burden, which is what was happening to Hannah. Your hopes for your teen must not be perceived as demands or expectations that your child feels incapable of fulfilling. When that happens, teens feel they have little choice, and they typically respond by becoming either depressed and self-destructive or rebellious and hence combative, as Hannah did.

Hannah's grades worsened, she became more and more lack-adaisical about her schoolwork, more and more preoccupied with how she looked—and more and more rebellious. She stayed up so late at night sending e-mails to friends that her mother had to nag her every morning to get up. As a result, she was often late for school. The more her parents pressured her, the less she did.

■   ■   ■

Hannah was what I call a *hothouse* child, by which I mean her parents were raising her as if she were some rare flower rather than a child who needed to discover an identity and a direction for herself based on what she perceived were her talents and possibilities. Thus, the school they had chosen was their hothouse and their hovering was akin to forcing light, water, and fertilizer on their exotic plant.

Communication between Hannah and her parents, particularly her mother, with whom she had been very close as a child, had all but broken down by the time she turned sixteen. What seemed rosy to them was anything but rosy to their daughter. On the contrary, Hannah had gone from a child who loved learning and felt good about herself, to a teenager who felt that she was in the "bottom fifty percent" in terms of attractiveness, popularity, intelligence, and talent. As she surveyed her social landscape she believed she could identify those students who would go on to become "stars" in one way or another; and she did not count herself among them.

In addition to their other disappointments, her parents were frustrated and angry, and even a little embarrassed by her flair for the unconventional, which Hannah suspected and resented. Any time her parents talked to her, she'd get angry and defensive. In the end, she seemed constantly hostile and testy.

Helping Your Combative Teen Achieve a Positive Identity

To understand what causes rebellious behavior in your child, you need to look for the underlying identity that drives her or him. As a rule, combative behavior reflects an emerging identity.

Hannah's identity was becoming that of a "rebel." Since she believed she could not compete effectively and carve out an identity as a "genius," she chose to define herself in opposition. This same process is often at work among siblings, especially among same-sex siblings where the older one is very successful and well behaved. If the younger sibling perceives that he or she can't compete on the playing field of achievement, that child may elect to become a rebel. For parents, this is both the bad news and the good news.

First, the bad news: You cannot force your child to want to compete unless he or she sees this as a viable option. Moreover, teens need to see this for themselves. Telling a teen that she or he is intelligent, or talented, is certainly not a bad thing for a parent to do, but expecting them to believe this just because you say it isn't reasonable. Similarly, your teen will not engage in competition—at least not wholeheartedly—unless she or he believes in her or his own potential to succeed. There is nothing sadder than watching a parent trying to cajole (or berate) a child into competing, when the child obviously doesn't want to.

Hannah knew very well that her parents expected her to make up for her brother's underachievement, by being a resounding success. Even if she thought this was possible, it was an unfair burden. If she acquiesced, she'd be living a life that her parents had designed for her, not her own life. Eventually, this would lead to trouble. As it was, given the school Hannah attended, being *resoundingly* successful was a tall order. She knew that simple success—getting decent if not outstanding grades—would not satisfy her parents, and, therefore, she would come up short in their eyes. If this were a boxing match, she would choose not to enter the ring. By pressuring her,

Hannah's parents were further undermining her shaky self-confidence and building a wall between them.

Now, the good news: While it may not be possible to stop a teen from seeing him- or herself as a rebel, it is possible to help steer that identity in a positive direction. Remember that another way to look at a rebel is as an "individual." Artists are often rebels to some degree, as are writers and journalists, and architects. Even lawyers can have a rebellious identity; they usually specialize in certain areas of the law, such as environmental law or educational law. If you child is developing an identity as a rebel, there's no need to set off alarms. However, to help steer your child toward a *healthy* rebel identity, you first need to lessen any tension that has built up in your relationship. In Hannah's case, this tension was intense.

NORMALIZING OPPOSITIONAL BEHAVIOR

Oppositional behavior usually escalates when parents overreact and try to suppress it. You should not be surprised when your teenager argues, confronts, or even opposes you. On the contrary, there may be more reason to worry if your teen is too compliant. You have to wonder why your child doesn't ever see anything to argue about. Is he or she too intimidated by you? Does your child suffer from a severe lack of confidence?

The need to argue about things—not necessarily in a hostile way—is essential to healthy identity development, and you should not only expect it, but also encourage it, especially if this arguing follows some rules, such as:

- No name-calling.

- No making threats if you or your child doesn't capitulate.

- No screaming.

- Listening to one another before responding.

- Assuming that your opponent's point of view makes sense to the person propounding it.

This type of normal arguing didn't occur between Hannah and her parents. In any discussion of what she was doing or ought to do, Hannah felt overwhelmed by them. Her father would not hesitate to literally shout her down. Her mother was quieter but no less relentless in verbalizing her expectations. Their constant refrain was that she should be a straight A student, especially in math and science, that she was wasting her talents by not practicing the piano, that she should be reading the great classics instead of emailing her friends, and so on. No matter what she tried to say, they would not hear her out. Eventually she concluded that they were not interested in how she saw things, were convinced that they were right, and determined that she bend to their will.

In the face of this, Hannah simply shut down verbally, but showed her opposition to their desires through her behavior. Since there was no room for healthy arguing between Hannah and her parents, in Hannah's mind it made perfect sense to avoid arguing, and instead, to go off in her own direction, in search of her own identity.

> **HEADS UP!** *Your child was not born to live up to your expectations.*

It's okay to have hopes for your teenager. It's okay to praise her or him. It's okay to point out your child's talents, and it's okay to support and nurture her or his interests. It is *not* okay to try to impose your will on your child. Your aspirations for your child, no matter how noble, will only complicate a teen's search for an identity. If you push for your expectations too aggressively, you can count on a breakdown of parent-teen communication. If somehow you do succeed in imposing your will on your child, years from now, the adult may discover that he or she is not leading his or her own life, but one of your design. This could precipitate an identity crisis the outcome of which is very uncertain.

To end the stalemate that was driving Hannah's decline, her parents needed to change the way they interacted with her. Hannah's father found this difficult to do, and kept harping at her, but her mother was more open to calling a truce. She hated the way she and her daughter had become alienated from one another, and felt trapped in the role of monitor and nag. What's more, she realized that what she and her husband had been doing was obviously not working.

As a result, Hannah's mother stopped asking about her schoolwork and instead started inviting her to do things together just for fun. She made a deliberate effort to talk less and listen more, and was soon rewarded with a growing understanding of how Hannah saw herself and her world. It was an abrupt shift, and at first Hannah was suspicious, but she loved to shop, and couldn't resist the invitations. On these expeditions, much to Hannah's surprise, her mother talked only about clothing, including what she had liked to wear as a teenager.

The turning point for Hannah came when her mother said without a hint of criticism, "I think you're coming to see yourself as something of a rebel, a nonconformer." It was evident to Hannah that her mother accepted the idea; and, after that, she started opening up about what life had been like for her since she'd started at the private school.

A little later Hannah's mother offered Hannah the *option* of transferring to the local public high school, and made it clear that this was not a punishment or a sign of failure, but Hannah's choice. She was prepared to buck her husband if necessary, but he had noticed a positive change in Hannah's overall demeanor, and decided that he would back off and let his wife take the lead.

HANNAH TODAY

Hannah is now in her senior year of high school. She opted to stay in the private school. She also decided to revisit her childhood passion for art. Painting and sculpture are her strongest interests, but she has also shown an interest in art history, especially Renaissance art. She has chosen a two-week vacation with her parents to Florence and Rome as her graduation present. She plans to spend a lot of time in the museums there. She still has not played the piano competitively, although she does play for her own entertainment, and occasionally for friends at parties. She plans to attend the state university, which has a good art school, but is not sure of her long-range plans. However, she identifies herself as an artist, more specifically as a painter. She remains unconventional and creative in her personal appearance.

Guiding Your Teen . . . From Combat to Healthy Rebellion

Parents need to embrace some humility. Rather than trying to turn your child into a hothouse plant, you will be better off providing the raw materials needed for healthy growth: love and kindness, openness and generosity, reasonable limits, and a role model of someone whose actions are consistent with his or her stated values. Having done this, we must then put our faith in our children to discover a healthy identity for themselves.

Hannah's mother's approach is an example of how you can channel a budding combatant in a positive direction.

SEVEN GUIDELINES TO HELP YOUR TEEN OVERCOME COMBATIVENESS

Guideline #1: Remember that moving toward being a rebel is not uncommon. A rebellious identity makes sense from the point of view of a combative teenager, if, for example, they feel they can't compete effectively with an older sibling or their peers. If you've never seen the movie *Rebel Without a Cause* starring James Dean, I suggest you watch it, preferably with your teenager. If you have seen it, watch it again. Rebelliousness may seem nonsensical to you, but teens have always romanticized it. An identity as a rebel may be very attractive to a teen, particularly one who is having a hard time finding a niche in life, or one who feels that he or she can't compete effectively with an older sibling or peers.

Guideline #2: Don't believe that arguing with your teen will make him or her more compliant. To get your teenager to give up oppositional or argumentative behavior, it's important to avoid encouraging it, which taking the bait too often and continual arguments can do. Learn to choose your battles. For example, if you've set a limit and are comfortable with it, don't allow yourself to be drawn into an ongoing battle over it. I suggest you listen—once—to your teen's arguments, and then if you decide to keep the limit as it is, let him or her know that the time for debate is over, period.

Guideline #3: Listen and learn how your teenager sees him- or herself and the world. Keeping the lines of communication open is best done by learning to listen without jumping in with unsolicited advice. Instead, ask your teen to talk more about how he or she views a particular situation, what options she or he sees for dealing with it, and what he or she is inclined to do. That way you will be able to see the world through your teen's eyes, and his or her emerging identity will reveal itself.

Guideline #4: Reduce the tension between you and your teenager. Calling a truce and accept that what your child is doing makes sense to her or him, even if it doesn't to you or the teachers.

Guideline #5: Put a name—rebel—to the identity that your teenager seems to be moving toward. Let him or her know that the world has seen many successful rebels, and that rebels are often responsible for important social changes. Remember Rosa Parks, the African-American woman who refused to take a seat at the back of the bus? In her quiet but determined way, she was a rebel.

Guideline #6: Let your teen know that you support being unconventional. At the same that you indicate that you can respect being unconventional, let your child know there are certain basic personal qualities, such as compassion, altruism, perseverance, and generosity, that you also respect.

Guideline # 7: Don't give in to the temptation to label your combative teen as mentally ill. Some psychiatric "diagnoses", such as "oppositional-defiant disorder" and "conduct disorder" really refer only to behavior problems. They do not represent some underlying abnormality in brain chemistry the way other diagnoses, like "schizophrenia" and "bipolar disorder" do. You need to think in terms of how behavior reflects identity, not brain chemistry.

FAQs

Q: If teenagers have an innate drive to test limits and argue, then aren't I harming my child by not arguing back?

A: It's best to not take the bait when your teen finds fault in everything you do or say. Try to maintain perspective. You can express your opinion, just as you need to define limits, but you can do this without implying that your teenager is crazy or weird, and without being drawn into a long, ongoing battle of ideas, or a debate about the appropriateness of a limit. Most parents can learn to tolerate a certain amount of limit-testing and oppositional behavior with good humor; you will need to find your own comfort zone. It is important to remember that no tolerance for argument is just as limiting to your child's development as unlimited tolerance for argument.

Q: My teenager is very good at arguing and often makes me feel that I'm wrong. Should I avoid arguing altogether?

A: No. If the outcome of these confrontations is that you always feel in the wrong, you need to take a good hard look at yourself to determine why you are so insecure, and you may need to look for some help. Talk to other parents to see how they handle similar situations. (In some cases, you may need the help of a counselor.) See how the limits you set compare to theirs and for help "validating" your ideas. The worst outcome of a disagreement between you and your teenager should be an agreement to disagree, and, when it comes to limits, the limit you set should stand even as you respectfully recognize your teen's right to disagree.

Q: So, when _do_ I give in to my teenager's arguments? Never?
A: No, not never, but not all the time, either. This is where respecting a teen's right to disagree comes into play. When you are able to establish a pattern of open and honest communication—avoiding a too rigid or too open-ended approach—you may at times be persuaded to agree with your child. This is not the end of the world so long as it doesn't happen all the time. The very process of establishing rules for appropriate parent–teen debate will help your son or daughter develop an identity as an effective person who is able to get at least some of what he or she wants. For teens: 1) never getting anything they want (and feeling ineffectual), and 2) getting what they want all the time, may both lead to dysfunctional identities.

Q: Whenever I try to talk to my daughter about a decision she's made, she blows up at me. What should I do?
A: This is the time for some honest self-examination. If your daughter always explodes when you try talking to her, chances are that you have established one of two patterns in the relationship: you are either being too rigid and trying to impose your will on her or you may have failed to set limits soon enough and now she cannot accept any limitations. If you've fallen into either one of these patterns, you have to face that fact and recognize that you have your work cut out for you.

6

helping your child build a resilient identity

MOST PARENTS want to know what exactly a "healthy"—or what I call a *resilient*—identity is, and to distinguish it from an unhealthy or *fragile* identity. To arrive at a description of these differences, researchers divided adults into two groups: the first, the "fragile" group, composed of those who were inclined to respond to stress by getting sick, mentally, physically, or both. The second, the resilient group, consisted of those who were able to remain mentally and physically healthy even when life wasn't going well.

Characteristics of a Resilient or Fragile Identity

As applied to teenagers, the most important differences between resilient and fragile identities include:

RESILIENT	FRAGILE
• Aware of personal *talents* and *abilities*.	• Aware of personal *limitations* and failures.
• *Accepts* personal limitations.	• *Ashamed* of personal limitations.
• *Enjoys* challenges and new experiences.	• *Fears* challenges, avoids new experiences.
• *Persists* in the face of difficulty or frustration.	• *Gives up* easily.
• *Optimistic.*	• *Pessimistic.*
• Generally *happy* and *friendly.*	• *Angry* or *depressed* much of the time.
• *Respects* adults.	• *Alienated* from adults.
• Tends to be a *leader* or an "individual."	• Tends to be a *follower* or an "outsider."
• *Trusts* others.	• *Distrusts* others.
• Believes life has *meaning* and *purpose.*	• Sees *little meaning* or *purpose* in life.
• Able to *prioritize* needs and desires and willingly makes sacrifices at times.	• Tends to perceive all needs and desires as *equal* and finds sacrifice painful.
• Regards personal crises as a *normal part of life* and does not take them personally.	• Tends to feel *victimized.*

Obviously, no teenager fits the description of fragile or resilient *all the time*. Don't be too hasty in making your assessment. Even teens with very resilient identities can feel depressed, anxious, or angry at times. Even the healthiest adolescent can feel discouraged at times, or get into conflict with the important adults in his or her life. On the other hand, resilient teens don't tend to stay stuck in their anxiety, depression, or anger, or allow conflict to fester until it becomes full-blown alienation.

Where does your teen fall in each of these categories? The more your child appears to be moving toward a fragile identity, the more likely it is that she or he may suffer from depression or anxiety, or become alienated and hostile. Embracing a fragile identity lessens the chance that your child will become a happy and physically healthy adult, who enjoys life and realizes his or her potential. Therefore, by guiding your teenager toward a resilient identity you are helping him or her to remain physically and mentally healthy for a lifetime.

Reality Check: Jumpback Jeff

Jeff, age seventeen and a high school senior, is a strapping six-footer with a quick smile and handsome dark looks. When he was nine years old, Jeff's parents went through a nasty divorce. His father, who clearly preferred playing golf to family life, and who'd had a minimal relationship with Jeff until the divorce, nevertheless sued for joint custody and a fifty-fifty residency arrangement, which meant Jeff had to divide his time equally between his parents' homes. Jeff eventually came to see the arrangement as a move motivated solely by financial concerns on the part of his father, because his dad remained as uninvolved in his life as ever. Still, Jeff felt he had no choice but to put up with it. After three years, he finally confronted his father, who simply said to the twelve-year-old, "If you don't like it here, don't stay."

At the beginning of his freshman year in high school, and now living with his mother, Jeff found himself the target of a group who thought he was of Middle-Eastern descent, and decided to take their prejudices out on him. This, of course, made him pretty miserable. Finally he told his mother, who arranged a series of meetings with school administrators and brought the issue of bullying to the PTO. She was determined to see to it that the problem wasn't ignored. She didn't think any child should be subject to bullying, and she insisted that corrective actions be directed at the student body as a whole, so that Jeff would not be singled out. Within a month, she had mobilized the community and the school. A stiff anti-bullying policy was adopted, teachers were given in-service training, and students were informed about the policy, as well as the consequences for being caught. After several students were caught and punished, the problem subsided.

At about the same time, Jeff confronted one of the bullies one on one and dared him to fight. Perhaps because of Jeff's size, the bully backed down.

JEFF TODAY

As stressful as these crises were, Jeff survived them. In fact, he did much better than just survive. He made his school's varsity football and baseball teams, and recently he received an acceptance letter from the college that was his first choice. He works out regularly, does not drink or use drugs, and for the past year has had a girlfriend who will be going to the same college as he will. His outlook on the future is bright. When asked to talk about himself he blushes slightly and demurs, but it is obvious that he is not ashamed of himself or his accomplishments.

Resilient Parent, Resilient Child

What accounts for Jeff's healthy identity? His parents' divorce and the divided lifestyle it led to could be considered traumatic. What made him different from Ian or Ryan? Well, for one thing, whereas Ian and Ryan had struggled and found it difficult to identify with the "winners" among their peers, Jeff experienced a lot of academic success, and he was also encouraged by his mom to develop his athletic talents. However, the factor that influenced him most was his mother, Judy.

Jeff and his younger sister were raised pretty much by Judy on her salary as a teacher; she received minimal support from their father. Jeff does not like to talk about the divorce, or the years when he and his sister had to shuttle back and forth. "I just think of it as something bad that happened, but that's in the past now. No point in dwelling on it."

Judy never talked to the children about what was going on between her and her husband, and Jeff admitted that he was glad she didn't. He recalled many times, though, even before his parents split up, when he could tell that his mother had been crying. "My dad can be a very critical person," Jeff explained, "and I've learned to take a lot of what he says with a big grain of salt. I don't think that was so easy for my mom to do, though. She doesn't talk about it, but I don't think he treated her very well. And he's always been the kind of person who takes care of himself first. For example, he told my mother he couldn't help pay for summer camp for us, but then bought himself a new golf cart."

Judy is a responsible, hardworking woman, but there is a great deal more to her than that. For one thing, she likes challenges. Although she loved classroom teaching, she also believed that she could help more children by shaping their educational experience. So, she continued her own education on a part-time basis, and in time she moved up, eventually achieving her goal of becoming an elementary school principal. She is an openly optimistic person who frequently voiced her faith in her own and her children's capacity to overcome adversity. She set strict limits for Jeff and his sister, but she was also their "chief cheerleader."

From the time they were infants, Judy was fiercely protective of her children, while also encouraging them to pursue activities and sports. She often told them, though, that she was less concerned with how well they performed, than she was with whether they were enjoying themselves. That enabled them to try new things without the fear of failing or disappointing her. Her daughter recalled her mother watching her play basketball in sixth grade. "Most of the other parents were screaming at their kids, telling them what to do. But my mother would always be laughing."

Judy's protectiveness kicked in whenever she perceived a threat to either of her children, as it did when Jeff was being bullied. There was a great deal of genuine affection and support in Judy's relationships with her children, but there were also limits and expectations. Judy would never ask her children to do something she believed they were not capable of; on the other hand, she always encouraged them to try things she believed they could do. She liked to laugh and have fun, and she made sure that both were a vital part of family life. Family activities were a regular part of weekend and summer life. Most of these were active things, like cross-country skiing in the winter and hiking in the summer. Judy monitored her children's schoolwork closely, and served as a resource as well as a source of support. She was consistently encouraging, positive, and patient, never giving them the impression that their work wasn't good enough or pressuring them to do things that she wanted them to do, as Hannah's parents had done. She set clear limits and enforced them, but she also allowed her children express their opinions and listened respectfully to them. If they could convince her—by the power of logic, not mere protest— to change a rule, grant a privilege, or soften a limit, she would do so.

LAYING A FOUNDATION

If finding an identity can be compared to building a house, then you can think of resilience as the foundation for that house. An identity that is built on a foundation that is fragile can't be expected to be as sturdy, or able to weather storms, as one that is built on a foundation that is resilient. People who have fragile identities are prone to anxiety or depression. They are intolerant and critical of themselves, and may also become aggressive as a result of their inner frustration.

As adolescents seek out identities of their own, they can't help but look around them at the identities of those who play a central role in their lives. Judy is a good example of how a parent who has a positive, resilient identity can influence her children to move in that same direction. Judy's own personality included many of the elements of resilience, including:

- Optimism: A belief in your own abilities and a hopeful outlook for the future.

- Purpose: A belief that life has meaning and that you were put here for a reason.

- Persistence: The ability to rise above failure and frustration and focus on what lies ahead, not what lies behind you.

- Challenge: The ability to find joy in testing your limits and trying new things.

The particular identity that your teenager eventually embraces will be unique to him or her. It will include a sense of who he or she is, why he or she is here, and what he or she wants from life. While you cannot answer such questions for your children, by revealing your own identity to them through your words and actions you can set the stage for what an identity can be, and show how it gives your life direction.

If your own identity is fragile, consider devoting yourself to strengthening that just as much as you do to parenting your teen. After all, what your adolescent sees when he or she looks at you can be as important as what he or she sees looking at him- or herself in the mirror.

> **HEADS UP!** *Don't panic.*

If your child appears to be developing an identity that is more fragile than resilient, it does not mean that the situation is hopeless. Quite the contrary, this insight can help you understand what you are dealing with and lead you to identify specific areas toward which you should be directing your efforts. The sooner you recognize signs of a fragile identity-in-progress, the more time you have to help your teen change course.

Guiding Your Teen . . . Away from a Fragile Identity

Unlike in previous chapters, where we offered several guidelines to help you put into practice what we "preached" in that chapter, here we have but one.

A SINGLE GUIDELINE: LOOK IN THE MIRROR

The best way to begin to steer your teenager away from a fragile identity and toward a more resilient one, is to take a look at yourself. Take a few minutes to reread the descriptions of resilient and fragile identities, only this time think about how much each one of them describes you. If you can see a fair amount of yourself in the definition of a fragile identity, then part of what you need to deal with has to do with modeling.

Guideline #1 and Only: To promote a resilient identity you have to be a model of a resilient identity. This requires honest reflection. To begin this process, take a personal inventory. If you have a partner, discuss it and share your thoughts about each other's identity. The idea of doing this may evoke some anxiety, but as long as you do not use this exercise as a means to find fault with one another, I guarantee that you will find this discussion illuminating. Use Exercise 6–1 as a guide.

Exercise 6–1: Parental Resilience Inventory

For each of the following statements consider how well you believe it describes you as you are today, from *0* (not at all) to *4* (very much). If you do this with a partner, also describe how well you think each statement describes the other person, and then discuss how you see yourselves and one another.

I enjoy taking on challenges that test my abilities.

<u>   </u> <u>   </u> <u>   </u> <u>   </u> <u>   </u>
 0   1   2   3   4

I believe that I was put on this earth for a purpose.

<u>   </u> <u>   </u> <u>   </u> <u>   </u> <u>   </u>
 0   1   2   3   4

I believe I can deal with any crisis that life deals me.

<u>   </u> <u>   </u> <u>   </u> <u>   </u> <u>   </u>
 0   1   2   3   4

I believe that crises and problems are a normal part of life and are to be expected.

<u>   </u> <u>   </u> <u>   </u> <u>   </u> <u>   </u>
 0   1   2   3   4

I am an optimistic person.

<u>   </u> <u>   </u> <u>   </u> <u>   </u> <u>   </u>
 0   1   2   3   4

I am aware of my talents and abilities and am proud of them.

<u>   </u> <u>   </u> <u>   </u> <u>   </u> <u>   </u>
 0   1   2   3   4

(continues)

Exercise 6–1: (continued)

I am happy most of the time.

| 0 | 1 | 2 | 3 | 4 |

I have a good sense of what's most important to me and don't mind making sacrifices based on my priorities.

| 0 | 1 | 2 | 3 | 4 |

I know my personal limitations and I feel okay about them.

| 0 | 1 | 2 | 3 | 4 |

I believe that people are trustworthy and that they try to do the right thing.

| 0 | 1 | 2 | 3 | 4 |

Now, total up your score, which can be anywhere from 0, meaning that none of these statements describe you at all, at least as you are today, to 40, meaning that all of the above statements describe you to a tee. The higher your score, the more resilient your identity is. Chances are that if your total score is high, you are someone who rarely if ever suffers from severe depression or debilitating anxiety. That's not to say that you are immune from all depression or anxiety; rather, it's that neither of these emotions takes over your life and you get over it in a reasonable time. Chances are that your physical health is also good, and that when you do get sick you recover quickly. You are upbeat and optimistic. Life doesn't get you down because you believe it has a purpose, and because you aren't afraid of challenges. Finally, you accept yourself, both for your abilities and talents and for your limitations. As the saying goes, you are comfortable in your own skin.

If you were to come up with a "wish list" for the kind of person you'd like your adolescent child to become, this would most likely capture it pretty well. Unfortunately, many parents don't experience themselves this way (or even close), but then are upset when their child's emerging identity doesn't measure up to their hopes. In reality, their teen's identity may resemble key aspects of their own identity!

FAQs

Q: Is it okay to try to have a conversation with my teenage son about things like optimism and the meaning of life? Won't he think that's weird?

A: Try it and see for yourself. My experience in working with teens is that they actually enjoy talking about things like the meaning of life and what their values and priorities are. Discussions about optimism versus pessimism can also be very interesting. The key to making these discussions work is to make them true dialogues, not one-sided monologues. Do at least as much listening as talking, and hear your teenager out.

Q: Isn't it dangerous to encourage teenagers to have too rosy a view of life? Aren't they bound to be disappointed?

A: I am not suggesting that you encourage your child to have an unrealistic view of life, or unrealistic expectations. Being resilient is not a matter of being naive or unrealistic. It amounts to seeing life as it is and accepting it, and being determined not to be defeated by the curves and crises that life throws at you. Being open about your own attitudes about life—optimism, persistence, and so on—and modeling these attitudes will provide your teenager with a solid foundation.

7

building healthy identities through adversity, challenge, and adventure

FOR A LONG TIME people believed that perseverance in the face of adversity built character. Perhaps the most well-known role model for this belief was Teddy Roosevelt. As a child, Roosevelt had been frail and sickly. He suffered from severe asthma, which, in the absence of our modern treatments, was often debilitating and occasionally deadly. Rather than giving in to his illness and developing an identity as a fragile individual with limited potential, Teddy, with the support of his family, pursued a rigorous regimen of daily exercise. He lifted weights and performed acrobatics on a horizontal bar. He persisted until he developed into a young man with a broad chest and a strong body.

In turn, Teddy's identity was rooted in these personal attributes, not in his asthma. In every aspect, his identity reflected the definition of resilience. As the rugged face carved into the side of Mount Rushmore attests, Teddy Roosevelt represents an enduring example of the virtue of perseverance in the face of adversity. To parents who believe this, the idea of insulating their children from life's difficulties and challenges makes no sense. On the contrary, they are inclined to believe that "coddling" children leads to an ineffective adulthood.

The pendulum has swung since Teddy Roosevelt's time, and many parents today attempt to shield their teenage children from any type of adversity. Of course, it's fine to stand up for your child, and to try your best to shelter him or her from truly traumatic experiences. In fact, protection of that sort is a parental obligation. But some parents may carry protection too far. They act as if they believe that their child should not have to persevere in the face of frustration, or cope with failure. In their efforts to smooth the road, they may inadvertently be promoting fragile identities.

Reality Check: Overprotected Owen

Owen, an eighteen-year-old high school senior, lacked any motivation to work in school. Ever since middle school he'd barely passed. As soon as anything became the least bit difficult, he would give up. Several times he had been moved on to the next grade simply because school officials found that easier than dealing with Owen's parents. Rather than presenting school as an introduction to life, complete with challenges, successes, and failures, they believed that school should be a totally positive experience, that it was the teachers' responsibility to motivate Owen by making school interesting and by creating "successful" experiences. The idea that learning could be frustrating at times (or even boring) violated their idea of what education should be. They actually thought that reducing school to fun and limiting education to a string of successes would lead Owen to a healthy and happy adulthood. That's not what happened.

When Owen refused to persevere even a little in the face of frustration, or when he simply refused to do something because he found it was boring, his parents put pressure the school instead of him. At one point, they insisted that he had learning disabilities. Later, they argued that their son was too intelligent for the curriculum, which was why he was bored and unmotivated. Last, they settled on the idea that Owen suffered from a mental illness that interfered with his ability to learn. Extensive testing at the school's expense uncovered no learning disabilities; Owen's intelligence was tested and found to be about average; and neither a psychologist nor a psychiatrist believe that Owen was mentally ill. Nevertheless, Owen's parents insisted that the school provide him with tutoring, allow him to skip work he simply neglected to do, and provide him ways to substitute different work for work he declared boring.

Now a senior, with graduation barely three months away, Owen was failing three of four courses, and had not even begun work on a mandatory senior project that he'd known about since the first day of that school year. After dragging Owen to three more doctors, they finally found one who diagnosed Owen as depressed and prescribed medication. While it is true that loss of motivation can be a symptom of depression, it did not make sense that this was the cause of Owen's dilemma. He didn't *lose* his motivation—he never had any. For years, he'd been shielded from any difficulty, his parents doing everything they could to smooth and soothe his passage through life.

Owen's parents continued to smooth out all the bumps right through graduation. They argued that Owen's depression meant that he would need special accommodations in order to be able to graduate. Instead of realizing their actions were undermining their son's identity development, they believed they were leveling the playing field between him and his peers. They were blind to the message—that Owen was in fact fragile—implicit in their actions.

Once more, rather than fight, school officials opted to compromise. Owen received a minimal assignment to complete as a senior project, and received far more assistance on it than any of his peers did. He was even given much easier substitute examinations in order to bring up his grades.

In the end, Owen graduated, and thus avoided having to repeat his senior year. Now, two years after graduating, Owen continues to live at home. He has had several jobs, all of which he was fired from, and currently works part-time at a restaurant as a prep chef, slicing vegetables and fruit. He cannot afford a car, or insurance for it, so his parents pay for both. They also give him gas money. His father believes that Owen regularly steals twenty dollars or so from his wallet, and his younger sister has accused him of raiding her savings as well. He has a girlfriend who works full-time while going to college part-time. He does not hesitate to take money from her as well. When his father confronted him and asked what he intended to do with his life, Owen replied that he was "thinking about" taking a course in filmmaking at a community college, but he hasn't done anything about that either.

The Problem with Overprotectiveness

Owen's story illustrates how a child's character can be undermined when parents go too far in shielding their children from adversity. Owen had settled on an identity that was dysfunctional in the extreme. Though he would never admit it, it was obvious that he viewed himself as someone incapable of standing on his own two feet (nor did he feel he had to). He was well on his way to being dependent on others forever. Although his parents saw the direction in which he was heading, they could not see the role they had played in guiding Owen in this direction.

I do not know if Owen's story has a happy ending. Owen's parents chose not to take my advice, which was to enroll him in an outdoor adventure program, so that he might experience the joy that comes from facing adversity and overcoming it. If Owen ever has that sort of experience, though, it could point the way toward a healthier identity.

THE CONNECTION BETWEEN CHARACTER AND IDENTITY

A resilient identity is what people usually mean when they describe a person as having character. Generally, they are also talking about someone who has learned to persevere in the face of adversity, and who has met challenges that have tested the limits of his or her talents and abilities. On reflection, it is difficult to think of someone you admire who has not faced adversity or who has not attempted significant challenges.

Sometimes when I look at children and teens, I wonder, *Whatever happened to adversity?* I'm surprised by how many parents seem determined to totally eliminate all difficulty from their children's lives, as if adversity will somehow weaken instead of strengthening them. While the intention is understandable, it is a very big mistake. Without some adversity, a child is apt to develop a fragile identity. The same applies to challenges—to testing the limits of a child's talents and abilities.

Experiencing success is important to healthy identity development, but that doesn't mean that you should never allow your child to fail. In order for success to boost self-confidence and promote resilience, your child must perceive it as legitimate. Even children as young as three can tell when their success has been faked, in which event it means little to them. Some believe that the best way to educate kids or help them develop healthy self-esteem is to pave their road in life with success after success. In my view, that does not work. Why? Because real life doesn't work that way. An approach based in reality, and which therefore includes failures as well as successes is more likely to lead to a healthy, resilient identity.

Am I advocating making life difficult for your child or teen? No, but I am advocating that you accept the fact that adversity is a normal part of life, and that attempting to completely shield your teenager from it is not in your child's best interest. You should encourage your child to test him- or herself and accept that this will sometimes lead to success, at other times failure. Remember as well that the effects of such failures are mitigated when your teen realizes that he or she made a genuine effort, and that success is rarely if ever achieved without some failure along the way.

Parenting is more art than science, and one important part of the art of parenting is to sense when adversity may become overwhelming to your child, and to intervene at that point to lessen it. As a rule, the younger the child, the fewer strategies they have to meet adversity. However, even the youngest children actually seek out challenge and adversity. If you doubt this, try the following experiment, as shown in Exercise 7–1:

Exercise 7–1: Observing Adversity and Challenge on the Playground

Ask your child or teenager (and your partner if you have one) to accompany you on a visit to a local school playground with swings, jungle gyms, and the like. Then, just observe the children and parents. I guarantee you that in half an hour you will observe all of the following:

- Even the youngest of toddlers will willingly test the limits of their abilities. They will *challenge* themselves. Some will push themselves with abandon, while others will show a measure of caution. However, few if any will not test themselves at all.

- You will see kids who are clearly experiencing both nervousness and intense excitement as they swing as high as they can, slide headfirst down the slides, climb rope ladders, and swing from bars several feet above the ground. Adversity is scary— but it's exciting as well.

- Some parents will be noticeably more comfortable than others with what their child is doing. Some will allow their children to play freely and set their own challenges. They will cheer their child on when he or she succeeds, offer helpful advice at times, and comfort their child if necessary if the child falls or gets bruised. Teddy Roosevelt's family was like that. Some parents, in contrast, will hover and be inclined to discourage their child from testing him or herself too much. You may also see a parent who actually pushes a child beyond that child's own comfort level. Finally, you may see one or two parents who fail to monitor their children at all, offering neither encouragement nor protection.

This exercise sums up at least one vital aspect of the art of parenting. Doing it may bring up memories of your own youth, and your approach to challenge and adversity. It is also a very useful tool for reflecting on your own parenting style. Which of the following would you say best describes your parenting style?

- *Laissez-Faire:* You don't interfere at all, one way or another, in your teen's life. You believe that the best way to raise your teenager is to let him or her make his or her own decisions, and experience the rewards of these efforts for him- or herself. You let your teen decide what if any challenges to take on, and do not protect or shield your child from any consequences or adversities he or she may encounter in life.

- *Moderate Coaching:* You support your child's decisions to take on challenges and even encourage him or her to do so. In the end, though, you leave the final decision to him or her. You offer advice or suggestions, but usually only when asked. You keep an eye out for potential problems, such as drugs, which might place your child or teen at risk, and you can even be aggressive at times about protecting your teenager when you perceive a dangerous situation brewing.

- *Aggressive Coaching:* You believe your teen should be strongly encouraged, even exhorted, to take on challenges and test the outside limits of her or his abilities. You believe that it is only by continually testing our limits that we can build character and self-esteem. You do not hesitate to offer advice and criticism; at the same time, you can be your child's biggest cheerleader.

- *Protective:* You are inclined to be cautious. You tend to be vigilant and will definitely discourage your child or teenager from taking on a challenge if in your opinion your child is not up to it. You believe that one of your responsibilities is to shield your child from failure. You are also inclined to shield your teenager from anything you regard as a potential hazard to physical or emotional health or safety.

You can probably find aspects of each of these styles in yourself. It can be difficult at times to resist an urge to hover or overprotect. On the other hand, you might sometimes want to press your kid— over his or her protest—to take on challenges that you believe would be good for her or him.

> **HEADS UP!** *Be a moderate coach.*

Although it is possible to make a cogent argument for every parenting style (and I've heard many such arguments over the years from parents who were truly passionate in their beliefs), I recommend that you strive to be the best coach you can be. What seems to work best, in my experience, is to place your faith in your teenager, to encourage and support, but to resist both the urge to press too much or to overprotect. This is truly an art.

> **HEADS UP!** *When it comes to punishment, less is more.*

REWARDS, PUNISHMENT, AND ADVERSITY

I am not a big advocate of rewards or punishment as a way of influencing teens or guiding them toward healthy identities. However, sometimes it is necessary for a parent to punish certain behavior—for example, in response to unprovoked aggression or bullying, or perhaps lying and stealing. However, keep this notion in mind: When it comes to punishment as a means of controlling teenagers, *less is more*.

If you find yourself *frequently* resorting to punishment in an effort to control your teenager, you're on the wrong track. Similarly, I see nothing wrong with rewarding teens now and then primarily as a means of acknowledging some achievement. But rewards are not the way to get teenagers to do something that parents want them to do but they don't want to do, like staying in school or following rules.

Again, if you find yourself frequently resorting to rewards in order to motivate a teen to do something, or to comply with some expectation of yours, you are on the wrong track.

Too much reliance on punishment to eliminate negative behavior, like too much reliance on reward to motivate good behavior, is likely to backfire. The more you rely on these things, the less effective they become. For this reason, my advice to parents of teens is always to choose your battles carefully and to dole out rewards thoughtfully.

Do not confuse adversity with punishment. Adversity is a *natural consequence of behavior*. For example, if a person sets a goal of running a four-minute mile, then the difficulty they encounter along the way to achieving this goal can be called *adversity*. Achieving a goal in the face of adversity builds *resilience*, or what is sometimes called strength of character.

Adversity can also be a negative consequence that flows from a teenager's decisions. For example, if your child chose to drive while intoxicated, and was arrested as a result, that would qualify as adversity. You need to be careful just how far you go to "smooth the bumps in the road" of your teenager's life. In such a situation, consider letting your teenager spend the night in jail, and then talk with her or him before making bail. In doing so you are not "punishing" your teen so much as allowing him to experience the natural consequences of his irresponsible behavior. If you decide to impose additional consequences, such as taking away the car or driving privileges, that would be punishment.

Similarly, if your teen is barred from sports as a natural consequence of poor academic performance, he or she is better served if you do not try to have this consequence lifted. Again, being disqualified is not a punishment, but a natural consequence. You could impose punishment on top of that consequence if you chose to. Whether you do so or not, it is better for a teen in this situation to face the adversity that is a consequence of her or his actions, and to do what is needed to restore her or his eligibility. This will promote resilience. In contrast, attempting to bend the rules or otherwise shield your child from having to face natural consequences and overcome adversity will only promote a fragile identity.

> **HEADS UP!** *Life is a country road, not a freeway.*

Thinking of life as a road that will inevitably have its smooth stretches as well as its bumpy stretches is a good thing to teach a child. Expecting life to be a smooth ride is a sure route to a fragile identity. Again, part of the art of parenting is deciding when to allow your teen to work her or his own way out of natural consequences and when (and how much) to intervene. There are no hard-and-fast rules, but you can use the coaching exercise earlier in this chapter as a guide to making such decisions.

Reality Check: Defective Dan

Engaging a teenager's sense of adventure is a great means of promoting healthy, resilient identity development. Ideally, it's best to start early, when a child is five or six. A child's sense of adventure is usually accessible at that age. However, even relatively conservative and cautious teens can often be lured into an adventure if it's done without too much pressure.

Dan was becoming a very cautious young man, partly because he had a hovering mother, Lois, who continually worried that he would get injured. This was not totally irrational. At age eight Dan was hit by a car while riding his bike and had sustained a significant head injury that led to a vulnerability to seizures and some permanent loss of vision in one eye. The seizures were brought under control with a low dose of medication. Through therapy, Dan was able to minimize his visual limitation.

Lois's general anxiety prompted her to deny him opportunities to do things that she thought were dangerous, and, unfortunately, an awful lot of things fell into that category. Her greatest fear was that Dan, who was now about to turn sixteen, would want to get his driver's license. She knew that car accidents were common among teenage drivers and had already told Dan that she did not want him to drive until he turned twenty. That led to a big argument, after which Lois reluctantly agreed that Dan could get his license and use the family car when he was eighteen, which was still two years later than most of his peers.

By this time, he had become pretty much a loner, and, eventually, he turned to drugs for recreation—first pot, then hallucinogens. They were readily available, and cost almost nothing. His weekly allowance was more than enough to keep him supplied. After a year of this, his grades had plummeted from As to Bs, then to Cs and Ds and finally to Fs. Lois got on his back about it, but it didn't make any difference. She was beginning to think that depression was the cause when Dan was caught with pot in his school backpack. When he admitted what (and how much) he'd been using, and for how long, Lois was floored.

> **HEADS UP!** Don't use mental illness as a way to deny the possibility that your teenager may be using drugs.

What to Do When Your Teen Is Doing Drugs

Parents are often the last people to think that their teenager is using drugs. Peers usually know it right away. Teachers may suspect it because they are able to observe not only a teen's academic work, but his or her social interactions. Regular drug users are inevitably observed in the company of known drug users. If they are social iso-lates, as Dan was, they may spend only as much time doing this as is necessary to get the drugs. On the other hand, if they have previ-ously developed a larger circle of friends, parents and teachers may notice that the teen spends less time with former friends in favor of a new group of friends.

The current trend is to interpret the effects of chronic drug use as symptoms of mental illness, particularly depression, bipolar dis-order, and attention deficit disorder. Although these mental illnesses do occur in adolescents, it is wise to first rule out drug abuse. *Drug abuse is more prevalent than mental illness among teens, and the effects of chronic drug use mimic the symptoms of mental illness.* A teen talking to a therapist, psychiatrist, or pediatrician is not going to be honest about the extent of his or her drug use. Most teens would sooner accept a psychiatric diagnosis than own up to their drug use. Many parents like Lois are astounded when they discover how long their child has been using drugs, and what drugs he or she has been using. When they do become aware of what's been going on, their teen's behavior finally makes sense to them.

When Dan's drug use finally did come out into the open, his mother did the right thing. While Dan, like most teens, minimized the problem, saying it was "no big deal," and tried to persuade his mother that he could just stop without any help, she saw the conse-quences that drugs had already had for her son and insisted that he enroll in a drug treatment program. Once in the program, and con-fronted by other youths who were essentially in the same boat together, Dan was able to admit to the extent of his drug use, how it had turned his life into a "train wreck", and how in spite of his protests and minimizing he knew he needed help. After being clean and sober for six months, and picking his grades up again, he went from the drug treatment program to a special track in the local high school, connected to the drug program and designed for teens like him, who had successfully "graduated" from the program. They met as a group three times a day: before classes started, at lunch, and again after classes ended for the day. Two counselors facilitated the meetings, at which the participants were able to talk about what was going on in their lives, both in and out of school. A condition of participation was random weekly drug tests. Another part of the program was regular group activities, which included things as simple as going to a nearby coffee house for coffee and dessert, to ice skating or going to a movie. Taken together, these activities with peers and interactions with staff constituted a new "culture" that Dan and the other youths became bonded to. It replaced their former peer groups, which had consisted exclusively of alienated and nonperforming youths who, like them, were entangled in drugs.

Dan had made some headway in breaking free from his social isolation through his participation in treatment and the special high school program. However, his self-image remained negative. He was very self-conscious and still saw himself as fairly inept, especially outside the classroom. He believed that he was unattractive to girls, and not very manly. Unless others took the initiative to draw him out, he remained alone. His recovery and academic success notwithstanding, Dan's still saw himself as defective.

It was at this point that the staff of the treatment program announced that there would be a weeklong "wilderness adventure" that would involve of camping out and a daylong river trip in inflatable boats. It was going to be Spartan: tents, sleeping bags, and cooking over wood fires.

It took the aid of the staff to persuade Lois to let him Dan go, but that camping trip ultimately helped Dan change his identity and, in turn, his life. At a slide presentation describing the wilderness adventure, Dan's mother saw her son in a new way: cooking breakfast for the group over a fire he'd helped make; washing up in a river; building a shelter from scratch. Last, but not least, she saw her son grinning broadly as he rode in the bow of an inflatable raft as it sailed through rapids, sending heavy spray back over his life jacket and helmeted head.

DAN TODAY

Dan had actually taken a leadership position among the group who participated in that wilderness adventure. Peers and staff alike recognized his hard work, and he was unanimously voted the person everyone most wanted to have along if they were ever stranded in the wilderness. His mother had the certificate framed, and it now hangs in their family room next to another framed picture: the photo of Dan going downriver.

Interestingly, the staff did not set out to change Dan's identity or to convince him that he was not defective. They merely *assumed* that he was not defective and related to him as they related to one another, never thinking that he was not capable of learning and mastering a skill.

Today Dan no longer thinks of himself as unattractive, unmanly, or defective. He will graduate from high school with honors. Administrators in the high school consider him such an important role model that he is scheduled to speak at graduation about his experience with drug abuse and recovery, and they have offered him a part-time job working as a teacher's aide while he attends a nearby college.

■ ■ ■

Encouraging your child to participate in wilderness experiences is one way to help your teenager see him- or herself in a new light, which could potentially to alter his or her sense of who he or she is in a positive way. You can have the same effect by incorporating elements of adventure into your family's life. One family, for example, has a tradition of taking annual summer vacations in Maine—one year camping out in one of Maine's many state forests, another renting a simple cabin on land bordering Acadia National Park. Every year, as the vacation drew nearer, the family spent time discussing what they would do that year. They had their favorite hiking trails, favorite mountain hikes, favorite places for boating, and so on. They also had favorite places to eat. During the vacation itself, each night they would gather around an open fire and finish the day talking about the day's activities, and making plans for the next day.

The tradition bound the family together. The adventure gave everyone an opportunity to experience new things. For example, as the children got older they opted to climb a new mountain together, meeting their parents back at the base after the climb. When one of the kids turned seventeen, he asked for a daylong lesson in rock climbing as a birthday present. The family gathered to watch him as, strapped into a harness, he learned to rappel down the side of a cliff. Obviously, this is a great experience in terms of positive identity development.

Guiding Your Teen . . . By Integrating Challenge and Adventure into your Family Life

Some of the specific things you can do to integrate challenge and adventure into your family's life in order to promote healthy identity development in your child:

TWO GUIDELINES TO HELP YOUR TEEN BUILD A HEALTHY IDENTITY THROUGH ADVENTURE

Guideline #1: Don't confuse challenge and adventure with vacationing. Vacations are fine, but a week at Disneyland or on a cruise ship is not the same as a weeklong wilderness adventure in which your child can learn survival skills and have an opportunity to learn something new about him- or herself. Neither is it the same as a week spent camping, hiking, boating, and cooking together. The kinds of shared experiences that bond a family tend to be those that include an element of challenge, not mere fun.

Guideline #2: Think "Less is More." Most Americans lead fairly complex lives. We own many more things than we need; in fact, our lives are fairly cluttered with them. We have cell phones that take pictures and send text messages or handheld devices that include a phone, Internet access, and e-mail. We have global positioning systems and satellite radio receivers in our cars. When we travel, we can watch a movie or listen to music on our MP3 players. At home we are likely to have at least one computer and access to hundreds of television stations, movies, and sports via a digital cable.

Imagine for a moment having these things taken away from your family. That would make many families very uncomfortable. Now think about what it would be like if your family *voluntarily* put those things aside in order to experience life from a different perspective. This is a simple yet very effective way to create an adventure and provide opportunities for your family to experience things that might otherwise pass them by. You might even experience yourselves in a different way.

FAQs

Q: Why do you advocate that parents be "moderate" coaches? What's wrong with pushing your child to do the very best he or she can?

A: Of course you want your child to realize his or her potential, but aggressive coaching only works when your teenager wants to take on the same challenge with the same measure of commitment that you have for him or her. However, you may not be able to separate what you want your child to achieve from your child's own goals. For this reason, if you want to adopt an aggressive coaching style you need to very careful that it is your child's goal, and not just your goal, that you are pursuing.

Otherwise, it will backfire. If your teenager does not embrace the goal, but gives in to your pressure and achieves the goal, he or she may ultimately experience it as your success. I have met adults who did this as teens, only to become disappointed adults who concluded that they had lived out their parents' idea of the good life, instead of their own, and have no idea of what kind of life *they* would want to live, and, therefore, end up very unhappy. And of course, if your teenager gives in to your pressure and does *not* achieve the goal, he or she will come to view him- or herself as a big disappointment. This kind of self-image is devastating, for all teens want to be admired and respected by their parents.

That's why I prefer to leave aggressive coaching to real sports coaches. If your teenager sets a goal and passionately wants to achieve it, then let him or her decide what kind of coaching works best. For example, say your teenage daughter sets a goal of playing basketball for a Division I NCAA university, in the hope of turning pro. You may feel comfortable supporting this challenge, but I'd advise you to let your daughter choose her own coach to help her get there. If she feels okay being pushed hard, fine, but don't try to be that coach yourself. Similarly, if your teen decides to become an attorney, it's appropriate for you to advise him or her that the road to that goal is a hard one. But don't turn into a demanding and critical law professor yourself!

Q: Does adventure have to involve wilderness?
A: No. On the other hand, I don't think a simple sightseeing vacation constitutes an adventure, because I don't believe that kind of experience is likely to open the way to new perspectives on self.

However, a trip abroad as part of a chaperoned group of teens, where your child is exposed to relative independence for the first time, would qualify as an adventure.

Q: Do you recommend wilderness experiences such as Outward Bound as therapy?

A: Yes. However, although you can send your teen to such a program, you really can't force her or him to participate. One teen who got a great deal out of a "therapeutic adventure" experience told me that while he decided to make the most of it, others spent most of their day in their sleeping bags. If you are concerned about the direction you see your teen's life heading in, and you can afford such a program—and if your child is willing—it can have a significant impact on your teen's emerging identity.

Q: How do you feel about boot camps for troubled teens?

A: Not good. For the most part, boot camps are places where oppositional and aggressive teens are sent. No matter how you describe it, your child knows he or she is being sent there either to be punished or "reformed." Many teens learn to modify their behavior to conform to the strict rules of a boot camp while they are there, but research has shown that the old, problem behaviors quickly reemerge once the teen returns home. In contrast to the essentially punitive atmosphere of a boot camp, a true adventure inspires excitement, not fear.

8

setting limits
establishing a family culture

SETTING AND ENFORCING reasonable limits is vital to healthy identity development in teenagers. In the absence of limits, an adolescent's identity is likely to become artificially inflated. A childhood and adolescence without reasonable limits breeds unrealistic expectations that can lead to a lifetime of frustration in work, relationships, and family life. It undermines motivation and the ability to persevere and find meaning in life. Here's an example of what can happen when there is a lack of appropriate limits.

The mayor of a city in one of our Mountain states was accompanying the local police on their nightly routes and tours. She was surprised at how many teens were being pulled over and arrested for driving while intoxicated, usually in the wee hours of the morning when she'd expected they would be in bed, asleep. More surprising was that these teenagers typically expected their parents to bail them out of their predicament, and in general did not seem to take being stopped or arrested too seriously. It was the mayor's impression that these teens did not expect any significant consequences. In my view, this pointed to some lax limits, which tend to promote an inflated identity in teens—almost a sense of being above the law.

The mayor then decided to visit with community groups and schools and set up a series of town hall meetings to discuss the issue of how parents were monitoring their teens. What she learned made her even more concerned. One high school principal, for example, told her that on more than one occasion he'd had to deal with parents who were outraged that their teenager had been disqualified from participating in varsity sports because of not just one, but *two* arrests for driving while intoxicated. Other parents of athletes complained that their teens about the amount of homework their child received, saying that it was interfering with their practice time! These and similar incidents were not especially rare, and reflected a more general attitude on the part of parents, which was that their children should not be denied participation in a pleasant activity because of either bad behavior or other responsibilities

Limits define the boundary that separates what we want from what we can have, and between what we want to do from what we can do. Your adolescent's identity development is at risk when the limits you set for her or him are either too restrictive or too lax. Teens who grow up within excessively rigid limits, meaning that they get little of what they want and rarely get to do what they'd like to do, are at risk of feeling insignificant. From their point of view, life may offer few opportunities and alternatives. They tend to feel small and entitled to little, if anything. They are apt to give up easily rather than persevere, to set their goals low, and to be unassertive. As adults, they are apt to get into relationships where they are used or abused.

At the other extreme are teens who grow up with few, if any, limits. As a result, they often think of themselves as the center of the universe. They feel entitled to *everything*. When life falls short of their expectations, they become angry and feel sorry for themselves. They, too, tend to give up easily, not because they feel small, but because they don't believe they should have to work hard for anything.

Teenagers love to argue and test limits; it's a normal part of their growing process. Therefore, every parent of a teen faces the task of setting and enforcing reasonable limits. For some, this can turn into a nightmare of ongoing conflict, but it doesn't have to be that way. Since rewards and punishments aren't as effective with teens as they are with younger children, the challenge you face is how to enforce limits on a teenager, and still give your child room to grow and discover who he or she is. For this reason, guiding your child toward a healthy identity requires a healthy *family culture*, which also makes the task of setting and enforcing limits less difficult.

Teenage Subculture

Our society has changed dramatically over the past few generations, largely because of rapid changes in technology. The result of that change is that today's teenagers live in a world of their own, which exists alongside adult culture but is largely unsupervised by it. This is a new cultural phenomenon, since historically and cross-culturally, adults closely monitored teenagers' lives. This new teen subculture, with its millions of members, is a major market for products and services, and a massive amount of advertising is aimed directly at it. It's fair to say that the overall effect of this constant exposure to the advertising machine is to promote a sense of over-entitlement among teens that parents are left to balance with financial realities and common sense.

Many parents don't know very much about the teen subculture. Occasionally, though, they become aware of some of its effects, as, for example, when they read a newspaper article about the incidence of unprotected sex among teens, watch a television news report about teenagers' increasing abuse of prescription drugs, or are confronted with the rampant problem of bullying or the latest school shooting. At these times, they realize just how little control they have over their teenager, and just how separate their world is from that of their child's. It hasn't always been this way.

How Tradition and Ritual Build Your Teen's Identity

Traditionally, all cultures, including our own, have recognized adolescence as a period of transition from childhood to adulthood. Native Americans, for example, recognizing that identity emerges out of adolescence and that the identity that a teen embraces can determine the course of his or her life, devised a rite of passage called the vision quest. Typically, this involved placing those adolescents who were preparing for it in the care of an experienced mentor (Medicine Man), who would prepare the teens for the rite and explain its purpose, which was to help them get in touch with their inner selves as well as their connection to Nature—in a word, with their *identity*.

At the same time as they prepared the youngsters for the quest, the mentors educated them about the tribe's expectations for them as adults, and about its other rites, rituals, and traditions. From the time they could walk, Native Americans immersed their children in a tribal culture that was rich in these rituals and traditions. Through mentoring and active participation in these rites, the tribe could to some extent control their youngsters' transition into adulthood. In effect, they were setting limits, while also recognizing the adolescent's need for individuality. Most important, by drawing youths into the culture, the tribe insured that the adolescent embraced an identity that included being a *vital part of* but not the *center of* the universe.

In Roman Catholicism, the rite of Confirmation traditionally marked a transition from childhood to adulthood. In order to be confirmed, adolescents were expected to learn a certain amount of Catholic teachings, and not unlike Native American teens, to choose their confirmation name. An analogous Jewish ritual is the Bar Mitzvah (for boys) and Bat Mitzvah (for girls). These rites are practiced today, although for many they have lost a lot of their power and relevance, particularly insofar as identity development is concerned.

Today, community culture as well as individual family culture is vanishing. In place of culture—organized rites, rituals, and traditions that are supervised by adults—a powerful adolescent subculture has evolved, and, it is in this context that teens are now finding their identities.

Hillary Clinton, in her book *It Takes a Village*, rightly argues that raising children is a community, not just a parental, responsibility. Earlier generations of parents could turn to extended family (grandparents, uncles, aunts, etc.), and sometimes even neighbors, to serve as extra pairs of eyes and ears—to extend their parental reach. Few parents could say that today.

In the past, cultures practiced rites of passage, provided mentors, and arranged for a broad network of supervision, all with the goal of teaching adolescents the rules of adult life and helping them develop identities in the context of the adult culture they would enter. Each family reflected the larger culture in addition to its own unique culture.

From a developmental perspective, the goal was to allow adolescents to carve out identities that would allow them their individuality—to believe that they are significant, but not the center of the universe—while also serving the community well. In that way each successive generation became the guardian of the culture's values, beliefs, and traditions. It created men and women who were in touch with and valued their individuality, but who also had a strong sense of belonging and responsibility to the community.

HEADS UP! *Pass on the rituals you grew up with.*

Think back on your childhood and what you know about your own parents' youth. Try to recall the rituals and traditions that your family practiced, as well as any rites of passage that you participated in. Exercise 8–1 will guide you through this journey through memory, and the effect that rituals and traditions had on you.

Exercise 8–1: Your Family Rituals

Take a moment to think about the traditions and rituals that were practiced in your family and community as you were growing up. Use these questions as your guide:

- *Which* if any holidays and occasions did your family celebrate?

- *How* did your family celebrate these occasions? For example, who was there? Was a meal part of the occasion? Were certain dishes typically part of the occasion, such as turkey on Thanksgiving, or a homemade cake for birthdays?

- What if any *rituals* did your family practice? For example, did your family have dinner together every Sunday, attend certain religious services together, go to the same place for a vacation every year, or watch the same holiday movie together every year? Rituals can also include daily habits such as saying grace before meals or reading stories at bedtime.

- Can you remember how you felt about your family's rituals and traditions? Did you look forward to any of them? What role did you and other family members play in these events?

As you reflect on those rituals and traditions that were a part of your youth, you may realize just how important they were to you. Even dysfunctional families can have rituals and traditions that bring them together. I have yet to meet a person whose upbringing was totally lacking in rituals and traditions who nevertheless felt that their family was cohesive. Rituals and traditions are the glue that keeps a family together

How to Create Your Family Culture

Many parents tell me that they feel isolated when dealing with their teenagers. Today, even the nuclear family may lack cohesiveness because both parents must work, leaving little time or energy to devote to traditions or rituals.

Like it or not, you need to face up to the reality that, because the community and extended family are not the resources they once were, it's up to you to set expectations for what is appropriate and acceptable behavior, and to guide your child toward a healthy identity. It's unrealistic to believe you can remove all forms of media from your home in order to insulate your teenager from the influence of the adolescent subculture. Instead, you have to devise some alternative strategies for setting limits and providing opportunities to embrace a healthy identity, while also giving your teen enough room to grow.

Part of a family's culture includes the limits they set for teens. This can't be done by sheer force of will. Teens have minds of their own. They have an innate drive to be independent. Teens wander further and longer, and they can't be effectively monitored twenty-four hours a day, seven days a week by even the most responsible parents.

However, the good news is that the following are all in your favor:

- Engaging children and teens in rituals and traditions helps build the parent-child bond.

- The parent-teen bond is much more effective than rewards and punishments when it comes to setting and enforcing reasonable limits.

- Rituals and traditions help shape identity because inherent in most rituals and traditions are certain values.

- Rituals and traditions also shape identity because they provide teens with a sense of their place in relation to the family and the community. They are an insurance policy against teens believing that they are the center of the universe.

David the Dad and Mark the Kid

When David's sons were midway through elementary school, he became interested in baking bread. It was a hobby; he hadn't planned that it would become the basis of a family ritual, it just turned out that way. Both of his boys were bread lovers. They clearly enjoyed the crusty loaves David slowly learned to make on Saturdays, and soon the bread became an integral part of hearty Sunday breakfasts. The family would sit around the kitchen table and feast on bacon, scrambled eggs, and thick slices of homemade toast slathered with butter and jam.

One day, the boys took sandwiches to school made from one of David's loaves, and came home raving about their much-improved lunches, and boasting about how their friends envied them their bounty, which, of course, pleased and encouraged David. Soon, he took complete responsibility for lunch making. His sons praised each successive improvement, which motivated him to add a mid-week round of baking to his schedule.

Things quickly moved beyond bread to carefully chosen luncheon meats, cheeses, and specialty mustards, not to mention calculations of the precise amount of unsalted creamery butter or mayonnaise that belonged on a sandwich. David began weekend searches for the best and most unusual deli meats, cheeses, varietal lettuces, peppers, cucumbers, various sprouts, and radishes. Often one or both of his sons accompanied him. Once he even spent two weeks experimenting to discover the best way to wrap a sandwich to maximize its freshness.

Sandwich making had grown into a family tradition—part of this family's *culture*. By the time the boys were in junior high, their classmates and even the faculty knew that theirs were the finest lunches known to man. The tradition continued all the way through high school. While they sometimes took their father's efforts for granted, they never stopped being appreciative.

The point of this story is not that a parent should bake bread and create custom lunches for his or her children; rather, it is to illustrate the importance or rituals and traditions to the healthy development of children. The point is that this father, through his baking and sandwich-making rituals, treated his sons as if they were special and deserved such treatment. At the same time, it strengthened their connection to him. This proved to be very important when the boys were in their junior and freshman years of high school respectively.

David's younger son, Mark, had found it a bit difficult—as many younger siblings do—to follow in his older brother's footsteps. Mark's older brother, Paul, was a standout athlete and a good student. He was heading off to college on an athletic scholarship, and already had a long-range goal to become a collegiate athletic director. He was also an extrovert who moved in a wide social circle. Occasionally, he'd party too hard and either come home drunk, or stay out all night, but there hadn't been many such occasions, and mostly Paul followed the rules.

Mark was also bright, though not nearly as drawn to or as talented at sports as his brother. His favorite subjects were science and English. He liked to read and write, and was also fascinated by nature. His favorite activities were hiking and writing poetry. In his freshman year in high school, he became interested in marijuana. Whereas Paul had always been pretty much of a straight arrow, Mark was intrigued by new things, which was probably why he started using pot, listening to music whose lyrics made David wince, and hanging out with kids whose futures did not look rosy.

David wanted to respect his younger son's individuality, but he did not like the direction he saw Mark taking. He understood that because Mark was an adolescent, he could not simply dictate what he did. Rather than engaging him in a head-to-head struggle, David decided that the best thing to do was to maintain the family rituals and traditions, to keep Mark engaged, and to make his opinions known without "telling" Mark that he was all wrong.

David felt he did need to establish some limits with Mark, about such things as letting his parents know where he was (or was going), checking in when he was going to be late, and having a curfew on school nights. They discussed these things, and even debated them; yet all the while, Sunday breakfasts and the specialty sandwiches continued. Mark would even go shopping with his father and the two of them would sit over coffee debating the wisdom of curfews or the legalization of marijuana. David expressed his opinions, but also listened to his son's arguments. In turn, Mark, although not perfect, generally checked in and came home on time. Their ritual had created mutual respect and caring that was stronger than the influence of the subculture Mark had joined.

HEADS UP! Make one night a week Pasta Night.

Ben and Carol

Ben and Carol, parents of three, found a great way to introduce ritual and tradition into their family life to so that adolescence would not to dilute the bond between them and their children. As their kids moved into middle school and junior high school it became apparent that between all of the various activities they were interested in it was more and more difficult to "synchronize" schedules in order to all be together at the same time. This is a common dilemma. Just keeping up with your kids' complex schedules can be a daunting task.

Ben and Carol were concerned that as important as their children's activities were, they came at the price of losing the sense of connection that was once so strong between them and the kids. They decided to declare Wednesday night "pasta night." Every Wednesday afternoon from five to six the family would be together to share a pasta meal. Their kids were welcome to invite a friend over, or to ask a visiting friend to stay for dinner. Attendance, however, was mandatory, even if that meant sacrificing an activity.

Pasta night was a great success, so much so that ten years later, after all their children had moved out of the house, pasta night continued to draw a regular crowd every week. It starts later now—at six instead of five—and it has been supplemented by Sunday brunch on the first Sunday of every month. The crowd now includes children, friends, and boyfriends and girlfriends. As they look back on it, pasta night was one of the best things Ben and Carol believe they did for their children.

How Rituals and Traditions Build Ties That Bind

David and Mark are a good example of the power of family rituals and traditions. Establishing and maintaining such rituals can give you many advantages. The first is that they serve as a counterbalance to the potent adolescent subculture. They help to keep your teen connected to you and your family, even when your child appears to be drifting in a dangerous direction, or influenced by marketing forces that you find objectionable. Traditions and rituals, such as those David created, have implied values—in this case caring for others, and being a nurturing person, which were integral to the family rituals. In addition, observing rituals and traditions is one way to keep communication channels open. Finally, the connection that rituals and traditions help you build with your child can give you a leg up when it comes to establishing rules and limits. In contrast, the less of a connection you have to your teenager—and vice versa—the more difficult it is to set limits.

> **HEADS UP!** *Hang in there!*

Your influence with your teenager will be enhanced to the extent that he or she feels bonded to you, and this connection is much more powerful than any reward you might offer or punishment you might threaten to impose to get a teen to do what you want. If you stick with your family's rituals and traditions, you will eventually see for yourself just how potent an influence they can be.

Setting Limits by Example

Setting limits on teenagers is easy; it's enforcing them that's difficult. Even schools have trouble enforcing limits as simple as what pictures or messages are okay on a T-shirt, how revealing clothes can be, what jewelry can be worn, or what hairstyles are appropriate for a classroom. Parents typically face similar battles, especially when their teenager points to others who are doing what they want to do. When it comes to setting limits for teens, people sometimes talk about "community standards," but since "community" is all but gone in many places, you may find that you are left to fend for yourself.

When it comes to setting limits for teens, the place to begin is with a look in the mirror. Ask yourself the following questions:

- Is it reasonable for me to place limits on things like tattoos or body piercing if I've spent money on cosmetic surgery, or have tattoos or numerous body piercings of my own?

- Is it reasonable for me to want my teenager to be less materialistic if I can't resist the latest techno-gadget, just have to have the latest fashions, or can't wait to get that new car?

- Can I expect my teenager to avoid drugs if I use drugs regularly to help me relax or get to sleep?

- Can I expect my teenager to be financially responsible if I have a hard time controlling my own spending?

In order to enforce limits, you must show that you can live a happy life within limits yourself. When our children are young, they may be less aware of discrepancies between what we say and what we do. Not so for teens. You may not realize it, but the limits that your teenager is having hard time honoring are the very ones you are having a hard time with. Therefore, the first rule of setting limits is: *Do not expect your child to comply with limits if you cannot offer them a role model by doing so yourself.*

Think back on your own adolescence and how well your parents modeled self-restraint. After all, isn't that what setting limits is all about—helping our sons and daughters to become adults who can show self-restraint?

I can recall my own father taking me shopping for shoes. We did this about twice a year. He'd take me to the shoe store and we'd look at the shoes on display in the window. As a teen, I naturally wanted what was in style at the time: pointy, shiny black shoes with wafer thin soles and heels. As a member of the singer/songwriter Billy Joel generation, I also wanted tight chino pants, tight shirts, and an iridescent sport coat to wear to school dances.

Our shopping routine was familiar; in fact, it was one of our rituals. Instead of asking me which shoes I wanted and going in and buying them, my father would engage me in a kind of negotiation. I'd start by pointing to the pointiest, flimsiest pair of shoes in the window. My father would look at them, and then shake his head. "Too flimsy," he'd say, pointing to their soles and heels. "We'll be repairing them every month." Then, pointing to another pair, he'd say, "How about those?"

This went on until we settled on a compromise pair of shoes that was not quite as pointy and more durable than I would have wanted, but more stylish and less durable than my father no doubt would have chosen.

My father not only talked about being sensible and frugal, but also lived his life that way. He was never impulsive or extravagant, and so when he went shopping with me and went about the parental task of setting limits, my adolescent urge to resist the limits he set could only carry me so far. Furthermore, I felt bonded to him, because although my family was far from perfect, it was a family that was steeped in ritual and tradition, like the shoe-shopping ritual. My connection to my father combined with the role model he provided helped make setting limits on me a little easier. Although they did not cater to my whims, my clothes were acceptable among my peers, but did not put me out on the fringe. This approach can work for you, too, if you take the time to build a bond between yourself and your teenager, and if you provide a model for the kind of limits you are seeking to impose.

Individuality and Limit Setting

Looking back on my own adolescence, I can say with confidence that my father would not have been caught dead in pointy shoes and an iridescent jacket. Yet he never ridiculed my tastes, nor did he suggest that there was anything inherently wrong with my wanting these things. I believe this was because he recognized my need to be a teenager and to define myself. Although we never spoke about it in those terms, I sense now that he was aware of my own search for identity, and was not interested in stifling it so much as putting some boundaries around it. In his relationship with me, I never doubted that he believed I would be a success, even if he might disagree with some of my decisions. When it came time for me to buy my first car, his approach was similar. He told me that he and my mother would contribute a certain amount toward it; then he went with me to a couple of car dealerships, where we engaged in a negotiation not unlike our shoe-shopping ritual.

The way an adolescent thinks of him- or herself is heavily influenced by how he or she is treated. If you treat a teen as if he or she is crazy or incompetent, then he or she may very well fulfill these expectations. The difference between a self-respecting teen with a healthy identity and one who lacks self-respect and moves toward a dysfunctional identity may lie not so much in how she or he acts, but in how she or he is treated. Therefore, when setting limits remember that there is a vital process going on underneath the limit testing. That process is the search for an identity. It's important for you to learn to negotiate with your child so that you can impose limits without stifling your child's development or giving teen messages that you have limited or negative expectations for them.

Guiding Your Teen . . . With Rituals and Traditions

Parent-child bonds don't come out of thin air. There are specific things that parents can do that will help to build this bond. It isn't reasonable to expect your teenager to feel bonded to you just because you are his or her parent. Bonding requires action. Here are some things you can do.

FIVE GUIDELINES TO HELP YOU BUILD TIES TO YOUR TEEN

Guideline #1: Start early. If you wait until your son or daughter has entered adolescence to think about establishing traditions or rituals, you are starting too late. The bonds that keep families together, which can help immunize your child against the influence of the adolescent subculture, take time to develop. They need to begin in early childhood, and they need nurturing. Family ties can't simply be created overnight. If you postpone doing this until your kids are older—by which time they may be more connected to their peers than to you—you are likely to find them highly resistant to the idea of starting a family ritual or tradition. That doesn't mean it's too late, but you will have to expect resistance and persist despite it.

Guideline #2: Make your rituals and traditions fun. Rituals and traditions often bring religion to people's minds. While all organized religions observe rites, rituals, and traditions (which also serve to build the bond between believers and the religion), these are not necessarily fun. Of course, the most effective religious traditions are those that are both rich in meaning and fun.

The family rituals and traditions you create will be successful only if they are fun. That doesn't mean that they can't also be meaningful. David's bread-making rituals were surely fun, but they also carried with them certain values. Almost any pleasurable activity can become a family ritual and tradition. Elaborate and expensive experiences—family cruises or visits to Disney World, for example—usually can't occur very often, although, in some families, they could become an occasional *tradition*—an event that helps bond the family, but which doesn't happen often. Thanksgiving dinner and annual family vacations also fall into this category. Other traditions that seem to work well are getting the family together to celebrate birthdays (complete with a homemade cake!) and family reunions.

Rituals are experiences that happen more often. Rituals include such things as going to movies together, picnicking on summer weekends, having Sunday dinner (or Saturday breakfast) together, and (for children) reading bedtime stories. "Pasta night" is a family ritual. Rituals can also involve affection, such as a kiss goodbye, or saying "I love you" at the end of a phone conversation.

Guideline #3: Keep them simple. Just as expensive traditions can be difficult to maintain, so can complicated traditions and rituals. Because they occur less often, traditions may work even if they take more effort. One family I know, for example, holds a reunion every other year. The five families involved rotate responsibility for the planning. Keeping budgets in mind, the person doing the planning locates a resort that is centrally located, can accommodate children, and offers meals and a variety of activities. The reunions are always scheduled at a time when off-season rates can be obtained. The families then gather for a long weekend, from Friday to Monday. The children—there are fifteen in all—look forward to seeing their cousins, and the adults look forward to the opportunity to kick back, relax, and trade stories.

In contrast to traditions, rituals are best kept simple, so that they are easy to maintain. Things like the Sunday breakfasts that David created fall into this category, as do nightly bedtime stories. Children look forward to rituals, and as any parent can affirm, they will nag you if you forget them. Nightly bedtime stories are not appropriate for teens, but you can create other family rituals. Be creative as you think about adding new rituals to your family life or reinstating rituals that you've let slide. Take a look at what rituals other families follow, and see if any of these appeal to you.

Guideline #4: Keep at it! A one-time visit to Disney World does not constitute a family tradition, any more than having Sunday dinner together twice a year constitutes a family ritual. Given the pace of today's lifestyles, and the competing priorities you must contend with, it is easy to let rituals, much less traditions, fade from family life, but if you want to build a bond with your children, you can't afford to overlook this key element. It needs to remain a vital part of your family life, and one that does not end as children move into adolescence.

FAQs

Q: Do I have to practice self-denial in order to set an example for my teenager?

A: Self-denial? No. Self-restraint? Definitely yes. If you don't want your teenager to have inflated expectations about what he or she can have and do, then you must set an example. Prioritize the things you want and let your teen know what these priorities are. Then, when you do get something you've been looking forward to, celebrate it together. Let the whole family know you just got that iPod you've been saving up for this past year! Let them know when you've saved up enough for that family vacation you've been looking forward to! And don't go around with a long face when you can't have something you want right here and now!

Q: Most of my own family traditions centered around the religion that I was raised in, but I haven't practiced that religion in years. What should I do with my children?

A: Rituals and traditions do not have to center around an organized religion, or with religion at all. Saying grace before dinner is a great nondenominational ritual that expresses gratitude for what we have. Bedtime prayers are another. Parents who prefer not to include any mention of God in family life can invent other bedtime rituals for their children, or replace a prayer with a meditation at dinnertime. Sometimes, people who decide for one reason or another to leave the religion they grew up with often also abandon all the rituals and traditions they practiced. This does not have to be the case. Religious holiday traditions can be replaced by other days—birthdays, Thanksgiving, the Fourth of July, etc., and used as the basis for family traditions. The important thing is to build rituals and traditions into your family life, whether these are based in an organized religion or not.

Q: My teenager does not want to go to family functions. Should I force him to go?

A: I would indeed pressure teens to participate in family traditions. In this case, it sometimes helps to bring in reinforcements. I encourage grandparents, for example, to stay in touch with their teenage grandchildren. They shouldn't wait for them to call, but should call and tell them how much they are looking forward to seeing them on their birthday, or at the Fourth of July family barbecue. They should also ask them what they've been doing lately for fun. Similarly, uncles and aunts can pitch in and do the same thing. Teens may grumble, but I believe that they respond to being told that their presence matters to others. We have definitely diluted the extended family, which was once a powerful force for bonding families together. Teens' relationships with their grandparents, uncles, aunts, and cousins were once a much stronger force for family cohesiveness than they are today. This may leave you in the position of going one-on-one with your teenager. You can reverse this, if you take the time to communicate with extended family and ask for this help. You may even be able to help someone else in return!

Q: My teenage daughter constantly nags me for the latest in sneakers and brand label clothing she says her peers are wearing. I have a limited budget. How can I avoid the constant arguments I get into with her whenever we go shopping?

A: As you say, you live on a budget. Let your teen do the same. Empower her to make decisions about what she wants to buy, but within a budget that you determine. Say, for example, that you give her a $200 limit for new school clothes. If she chooses to buy one designer label t-shirt for $30, so be it. That leaves her $170 for whatever else she wants. Don't waste your time arguing or wagging your finger, or saying, "I told you so!" if she runs out of money before she's bought a pair of jeans. She will learn in time, as you have learned, to set priorities and make choices.

Q: What about tattoos, nose piercing, tongue piercing, and so on? Where do I draw the line?

A: The first place to draw a line is to decide at what age your child is able to make such decisions. After all, unlike your child's choice in apparel or music, these things are not transient. Tattoos are permanent, as are holes in her or his nose, tongue, or ears. Your decision about when to allow your child to make such decisions needs to be made as soon the issue comes up; therefore, you need to give this some thought ahead of time. Similar thought should be given to when to allow a teen to drive the family car and where they can drive it.

One mother decided on the following limits, which she expressed to her ten- and twelve-year-old daughters simultaneously: They could get their ears pierced (two in each ear if they liked) when they turned thirteen; but they could not get any other piercings until they were in their senior year in high school. For this mother, this was one of the few firm, no-room-for-negotiation limits she intended to set for her daughters. They knew it when she said it, and even though occasionally one of them would bring it up, it never became an issue. When it came to such things as makeup, hair color, jewelry, and clothing, this mother set fairly liberal limits. As long as they did not dress or groom themselves in ways that were blatantly sexually provocative, she was content to let them experiment (which they did!).

9

the unkindest cut
healing the self-destructive teen

THERE MAY BE nothing more disturbing than discovering that your teenager is being deliberately self-destructive. Sadly, such behavior is now pervasive among teens, especially if you count self-inflicted tattooing, although some self-tattooing may come from a simple desire to adorn oneself without having to pay for it. However, in most cases, self-destructive behavior—commonly referred to as "cutting"—offers clues to a teenager's emerging identity.

Reality Check: Tyler, Lynne and Jennifer: Three Teens, One Problem

Tyler, a high school junior, is tall, and thin, with chin-length blond hair that frequently flops over his eyes. He is a thoughtful young man, intelligent but shy. His passion is computer games, especially complex ones that he plays on the Internet; but he also enjoys hands-on activities like helping his father replace a broken well pump or build a shed. He is an A student, takes advanced courses, and expresses an interest in going to college to study meteorology. He is not particularly interested in athletics, has only a couple of friends (but talks to them regularly), and prefers spending time on his computer to watching television or movies. He spends hours a day at this, locked away in his room. He spends so much time on the computer that his parents sometimes wonder if they made a mistake getting the it in the first place; they ponder whether they should impose limits on its use. On the other hand, they know how much their son enjoys it and how little he really seems to enjoy anything else.

Tyler's parents became quite worried about him when they discovered a blog that he authors on his personal Web site. In it, he described deep feelings of depression and mentioned a series of scratches on his upper arms. When his mother asked about them, Tyler brushed her off, saying he'd scratched himself moving some things around in the basement. Soon after, though, Tyler's father got a call at work from the school principal, who told him that a teacher had noticed some blood on Tyler's T-shirt and sent him to see the school nurse, who found the cause: several deep scratches on Tyler's upper arm.

When Tyler's father arrived, the principal and nurse, as well as the school psychologist were waiting for him. Tyler was called in, but had little to say. He admitted cutting himself, denied that he had any suicidal intent, but couldn't really respond when asked why he'd done it. The school officials all strongly recommended that Tyler receive a psychiatric evaluation.

■　■　■

Lynne's parents were also quite worried about their teenager. It was only mid-October, but she had already missed nearly three weeks of school. It was her junior year, and since colleges tend to weigh junior year grades heavily when considering applications, it was extremely important that she do well. Even though the school sent work home, Lynne was already behind and struggling in several classes. She'd wake up in the morning and complain of stomach pain. Then she'd vomit. Although Lynne's parents took her to the doctor, they knew that she wasn't really sick, and weren't surprised when the doctor recommended counseling. His diagnosis was that Lynne, for some reason, had become school phobic, and that they needed to get to the root of her fears.

One morning, as Lynne and her mother were arguing about getting up and going to school, her mother noticed that both of Lynne's legs had long scratch tracks, which, although not deep, were both obvious and plentiful. When her mom asked about them, Lynne just shrugged. She didn't deny scratching herself; in fact, she admitted that she'd been doing it off and on for several months. Like Tyler, though, she really couldn't say why she'd done it.

As Lynne saw it, she wasn't *afraid* of school, she just *hated* it. Lynne, like Tyler, was shy. She was also soft-spoken, so much so that it was difficult for me, sitting not more than six feet away in a quiet office, at times to hear her clearly. When called on in class, Lynne would blush deeply and instantly become tongue-tied. Of course, she never raised her hand, and when teachers saw how pained she was, they tended not to call on her.

On the first day of school that year, Lynne's English teacher told the class that one of their assignments for the coming month was to make a five-minute oral book report.

Lynne immediately got sick to her stomach, dashed off to the bathroom, and vomited.

Lynne had no real friends at school. She just could not bring herself to start up conversations; and when others tried to start one, it was as if her tongue became paralyzed. She was too anxious to join clubs. Once, when she relented to pressure from her parents to sign up to play in an intramural softball league, she couldn't wait for the season to be over, although she turned out to be an okay player. Again, she did not make a single friend through this activity, and, at the end of each game, she'd hop on her bike and ride home the moment the last strike was called.

■ ■ ■

On the surface, fifteen-year-old Jennifer appeared to be very different from both Tyler and Lynne. Jennifer was a top student. She was active in athletics, as well as the school drama club. She had many friends and led a very active social life. Nevertheless, Jennifer had always believed that her older sister, Kate, was the family favorite. She also believed that Kate, who was tall and slender, was also more attractive. Jennifer was envious of Kate, and felt that she was doomed to be second best. This created a certain amount of tension between the sisters, which would sometimes spill over into the general atmosphere in the house. As obvious as it was, however, Jennifer's parents never talked about this sibling rivalry. They never explored it or tried to work it out. From their point of view they loved their daughters equally, and treated them equally. For some reason they treated the issue of jealousy as if it were a taboo not to be violated. For the past year, they had been having marital problems, and were in counseling. They didn't discuss that either, or even openly acknowledge it, despite the fact that both girls knew.

Because of all of her obvious assets, Jennifer's parents were stunned to discover that she was cutting herself. This happened when one of Jennifer's friends noticed some scratches on Jennifer's arm, and told a teacher. Her teachers also were shocked, because Jennifer seemed to them to be the least likely teenager to become a cutter.

Signs That Your Teen May Be a Cutter

Perhaps you recognize your teenager in one of these examples. Almost without exception, "cutters" tend to view themselves as unworthy, ineffectual, and with poor prospects for a happy future. Regardless of how they may appear on the surface, inside they are angry, depressed, or both. They don't really like themselves, and hurting themselves is a way to vent their feelings of anger or frustration. Their emerging identities tend toward fragile (see Chapter 6). The more you talk to them, the more apparent their fragility becomes. Signs that your child may be hurting him- or herself include:

Greater Awareness of Personal Limitations Than Abilities. Tyler, Lynne, and Jennifer were all much more aware of their perceived weaknesses and limitations than of any strengths and assets they possessed. No matter how successful Jennifer was in other people's eyes, in her own mind Kate would always be more popular than she. For his part, Tyler felt he was competent when it came to computers, but believed that no girl would want him for a boyfriend. And when Lynne looked in the mirror all she saw was faults, no strengths.

A Pessimistic Outlook. Neither their parents nor their teachers had any inkling that these teens were increasingly adopting a pessimistic outlook on life. Jennifer, for example, believed that her parents would divorce, and that any money they'd saved for her college education would disappear. She also believed that Kate would always be the family favorite, and that she would be a distant second in their eyes. Tyler buried himself in computer games in part because he liked them, but also because they allowed him to avoid coming to terms with his shyness. Shyness, of course, was a major issue for Lynne. She was very aware of her anxiety, and she believed that she was forever doomed to stand on the outside the window of life, looking in, rather than participating in it.

Easily Discouraged. This was truer of Lynne and Tyler than of Jennifer, although given Jennifer's perception that no matter what measure she used, she came up short when compared to Kate, she, too, might eventually lose some of her drive. She was a top student, but so had Kate been. She was active in sports as well as in her school's drama program, but so had Kate been. Moreover, Kate had gotten *lead* roles in plays and been named a team captain, while Jennifer had to settle for *supporting* roles and was not named captain. Her parents, who never openly compared their daughters, were oblivious to these feelings.

> **HEADS UP!** *Always look beyond the behavior to find the identity causing it.*

CUTTING: A SYMPTOM OF A DYSFUNCTIONAL IDENTITY IN THE MAKING

The first thing to remember should you discover that your teenager has become a cutter is that this points to an identity issue. Don't be caught up in guilt; you did not cause this behavior—and you can be part of the solution. You are not privy to everything your child feels, and your child may not be able to articulate exactly why she or he has been cutting. Cutting is a symptom—not of mental illness, but of a dysfunctional identity in the works. It is important, therefore, that the lines of communication with your teenager are kept open so that you are able to influence your child's identity as it emerges. It is okay to talk about the cutting, and to share your anxiety about it. At the same time, you need to look for a solution in your teenager's sense of who she or he is, how she or he fits into the scheme of things, and where she or he thinks her or his life is going.

Shyness and Identity Development

Although not all cutters are shy, more are than aren't. Shyness can have a definite impact on identity development. In children, shyness may be tolerated and may even appear cute, but in adolescents—and even more so in adults—shyness generally is a handicap.

BORN SHY

Shyness is something we are born with, not something your child chose. It is evident in children as young as three, and is associated with a limited tolerance for being looked at (an aversion to eye contact) and a heightened fear of strangers. Shy children are socially sensitive and react strongly to anger. Even the mildest criticism can make a shy child cry. In contrast, children who are naturally gregarious don't hesitate, for example, to approach strangers and introduce themselves, or approach children they don't know and ask them to play.

Both shyness and gregariousness can influence identity development. We all know whether we are shy or gregarious and we recognize these qualities in others. The key to how this affects identity development lies in whether we perceive our temperament as an asset (or at least acceptable) or a liability. Teens can easily come to see their shyness as a serious liability that limits their options for making friends and for meeting life head-on.

LOOKING FOR SHYNESS IN YOUR FAMILY TREE

Shyness and gregariousness tend to run in families. Not that everyone in a family is likely to be shy, but chances are that for every shy child there will be an equally shy family member—a parent, sibling, cousin, uncle, or aunt. The *outcome* of their shyness—whether this person was truly handicapped as a result or lived a happy and productive life despite it—can profoundly affect your teenager's attitude toward his or her own shyness and is well worth discussing. The message to your teenager should be that a person can't just wish shyness away, but neither does it have to become a handicap. Assess your situation with Exercise 9–1.

Exercise 9–1: Examine Yourself and Your Family

Take a moment to think about yourself, any brothers or sisters you may have, and your own parents. Can you identify a tendency toward shyness in any of these people? Would you describe yourself as shy, or were you the gregarious type? Use the following scale to rate your temperament on the shyness–gregariousness scale:

0	1	2	3	4	5	6	7	8	9	10
SHY										GREGARIOUS

Was shyness a problem for you when you were a child or adolescent? How about for other family members? If it was, in what ways was it limiting? How did you (or they) attempt to compensate for shyness? How well did these efforts work?

_____

_____

_____

_____

Describe your teenager's temperament using the same 10-point scale:

0   1   2   3   4   5   6   7   8   9   10
SHY   GREGARIOUS

Think about the questions below:

- Do you think shyness may be causing problems for your teen?

- If so, in what ways?

- Do you think shyness may be influencing your teen's view of her- or himself or of life in general?

- Do you think his or her life is limited in any way because of shyness?

> **HEADS UP!** *Don't jump to conclusions. Consider how shyness is affecting your child.*

Don't assume that shyness will be a handicap for your teenager, especially if you believe that his or her shyness score is a 4 or higher on the above scale. Conversely, you should not assume that shyness won't be a problem. Shy adults don't talk readily about their shyness because they're shy! The same is true for shy teens. They prefer to avoid talking about their shyness, simply because talking about it puts the spotlight on them, and they hate nothing more than being in the spotlight. If, however, you do more listening than talking, avoid telling your child what she or he ought to do, and follow the other communication guidelines outlined in this book, you will be able to gain some insight into just how big an issue shyness is for your child.

HOW SHYNESS INFLUENCES IDENTITY

Shyness, especially extreme shyness (scores of 0–2 on the scale, for example) can have a strong effect on your child's emerging identity. An extremely shy teenager is apt to feel like a real nobody. They often describe themselves as feeling socially invisible. Words such as "wallflower" and expressions like "fading into the wallpaper" have long been used to describe very shy people. If you are shy, you can probably relate to this, and perhaps even feel the pain of being invisible. If you are not particularly shy, imagine for a moment what it would be like to be in a room full of people and feel that you are *invisible*. Imagine the tension that might build up inside you, and how you might come to hate yourself. Under such circumstances, hurting yourself can well become a way to release the tension and to punish yourself for being a nobody. After cutting themselves, teens feel a sense of relief, an inner calm, and an end—at least temporarily—to anxiety.

HOW SHYNESS CAN LEAD TO SELF-HATRED

Shy teenagers tend to build up an awful lot of frustration, which they are inclined to keep to themselves, leaving them feeling isolated, alone with their discomfort. In time, they come to feel inferior, that they are somehow abnormal, missing something (gregariousness) that everyone else seems to have. In place of gregariousness, they are saddled with this awful social anxiety. These feelings, in turn, become a breeding ground for self-hatred. This was definitely true for Tyler and Lynne. They were extremely aware of their shyness and they hated themselves for it. They experienced the urge to cut themselves when they were alone and unable to distract themselves from these feelings of self-hate.

They avoided talking about their shyness with their parents, and they were too embarrassed to talk about it even to the few friends they had. They very much felt like outsiders among their peers.

They knew other teens who engaged in similar behavior (which is not surprising since cutting is in fact common today), so they were also aware that cutting is a behavior that some teenagers engage in. Cutting served two purposes: It provided a release for pent-up frustration, and it also was an outward manifestation of these teen's intense dislike of who they were.

SELF-HATRED AND SELF-DESTRUCTIVE BEHAVIOR

While shyness, isolation, and the sense of inferiority it creates contributed strongly to the cutting behavior of Tyler and Lynne, shyness was not so much the issue for Jennifer. What she did have in common with them, however, was self-hatred. Although the causes were different for all three of these teens, cutting became their final common pathway for releasing pent-up stress and anger.

Why would a girl like Jennifer, who seemed to have everything going for her, want to cut herself? Again, the answer lies not in how a teen looks from the outside, but what they are seeing from the inside. Jennifer was one of those teens who, faced with the challenge of growing up in the shadow of a talented older sibling of the same sex, instead of carving out a strikingly different identity (which is the more common outcome) tries to outdo their sister or brother. Often, no matter how hard they try, they come up short in their own eyes.

This was certainly true for Jennifer. Although Jennifer did not regard herself as a *nobody*, neither did she really see herself as a *somebody*, which she believed her sister was. No matter how attractive she was, for example, or how athletic, or academically successful, she never felt that she could quite measure up to her sister. Like Tyler and Lynne, she really didn't like who she was. And like them, she kept these feelings to herself. Those feelings, along with her fear that her parents might divorce, were enough to stoke the furnace of anger and frustration that found an outlet in Jennifer's cutting.

Tyler, Lynne, and Jennifer Today

Fortunately, the struggle to find a healthy identity—one that leads to self-esteem and optimism rather than depression, self-hatred, or alienation—ended happily for all three of these teens.

TYLER

Tyler's father noticed one day that Tyler had brought home a copy of the high school newspaper, and suggested that Tyler, with all his expertise in Internet computer games, think about writing a review of some of these games for the paper. Tyler was reticent at first, saying that he didn't know how to go about doing that and, in any event, wasn't sure that it would be well-received.

Tyler's father didn't want to put too much pressure on his son; on the other hand, he really did believe that Tyler could do a good job of this, and that contrary to Tyler's belief, many students would be interested in such a column. He also didn't consider it going too far to call the school principal and ask about the paper: who the editors were, what columns were being written, and so on. When the principal learned about Tyler's interest in complex computer games (as opposed to what are commonly called "first person shooter" games), he expressed great enthusiasm, and suggested that the editor approach Tyler to test his interest.

Tyler's first computer column, for which he chose the pseudonym The Game Geek, appeared in the next issue. Students quickly discovered who the game geek was, and Tyler instantly became a bit of a celebrity. Suddenly, being a "geek" was a status symbol. Although be was unaccustomed to being in the spotlight, and said that it made him somewhat uncomfortable, Tyler admitted that it was also enjoyable, and it wasn't hard for the editor to persuade him to continue writing the column.

For the final edition of that year's paper, he wrote a long article discussing the pros and cons of becoming involved in the Internet gaming scene. He even commented that a potential danger was Internet addiction!

LYNNE

Lynne's severe shyness was a clear risk to carving out a functional identity. As time went on, she felt more and more like a nobody. No matter how many times her mother or father encouraged her to participate in some social activity, for instance through their church, the community, or the fire department where they volunteered, she found an excuse not to pursue it. When they tried to coach her in social skills, she'd dig her heels in and throw a mini-fit. In time, they just threw their hands up and told themselves that their daughter would just have to find her own way, although they remained concerned about her continued attempt to come up with excuses not to go to school.

As it did for Tyler, opportunity knocked for Lynne. It happened when she went with her mother to an exhibit of puppets at a nearby university, one which offered a major in puppetry through its school of fine arts. Lynne found the puppets fascinating. They were much more elaborate and creative than she'd imagined, and her interest was immediately piqued. She was so interested, in fact, that she asked her mother if they could see the exhibit again the next weekend. Lynne's mother couldn't attend, but suggested that Lynne go alone, which she did. That experience, as it turned out, provided Lynne with an opening to a new identity.

When her mother came to fetch her, Lynne showed her a brochure she'd picked up, which described a puppet-making class that the department was offering, and asked if that could be one of her Christmas presents. Her mother was thrilled at Lynne's interest, and quickly agreed. In fact, she said, it didn't even have to be a Christmas present.

At the workshop, Lynne not only learned the basics of puppet making, but also something about puppetry. To her surprise, as the students introduced themselves in the first class, several others—including two adults and two teenagers—volunteered that they were shy. One of the adults also said that as a youth she'd had a stutter. According to Lynne, on hearing these things the instructor laughed and said, "Of course! Don't you know that some of the greatest puppeteers have been extremely shy people?" Hearing this, Lynne nearly fell off her chair.

Lynne has now built a number of puppets and performed in several puppet shows in local schools, nursing homes, libraries, and even the university. She plans to attend that university and pursue a career in puppetry. Although she still describes herself as a shy person, she now has a number of friends that she regularly talks to, and has even had some to her house as overnight guests.

JENNIFER

Once her parents ended their uncomfortable silence and began talking more openly about sibling jealousy, treating it as a normal fact of life instead of a taboo subject, the tension level in the house as well as between Jennifer and her older sister, diminished noticeably. Jennifer also seemed more relaxed and generally happier, though her parents were aware that there was still a strong competitive streak in their younger daughter, that she was inclined to drive herself and compare herself to others, and that she could be impatient and intolerant at times.

Then Jennifer unexpectedly discovered an outlet for her energy and creativity that had nothing to do with competition or comparing herself to her older sister. She discovered and explored an aspect of herself that opened the door to a richer, deeper, and ultimately more satisfying identity. As was true for Tyler and Lynne, the answer for Jennifer was surprisingly simple, yet amazingly powerful in its effect on her sense of who she was and what was important to her. Some might even call Jennifer's experience an epiphany, in that it altered her entire view of herself and the world.

It came one sunny day in early fall when she came home and found her mother and grandmother going through a cedar chest. The chest had been one of her grandmother's wedding gifts, but for as long as Jennifer could recall it sat in a corner of their spacious family room, covered with a cushion and used as a bench. That day, however, the chest was open and Jennifer's mother and grandmother were going through what must have been two dozen quilts. Though Jennifer knew that her grandmother was a quilter—indeed, that she had made quilts for all her grandchildren—Jennifer had not seen these quilts for years and had forgotten about them.

Now, Jennifer was entranced by them. She sat down beside her grandmother and asked about each quilt. Some particularly colorful and bold quilts, she learned, were based on traditional Quaker patterns. Others had been designed by her grandmother and had clearly discernable patterns. There were also "crazy quilts" with no discernable pattern made from random pieces of fabric cut into random sizes. These were fun to look at, and Jennifer found them especially pleasing.

After a while, Jennifer asked her mother and grandmother why they were going through the quilts. Her grandmother explained that she was still modestly active in a quilting group, and that the group had decided to make small quilts for each child who came to a local summer camp for children with cancer or other serious, chronic, and disabling medical conditions. Receiving their own unique quilt on arrival was one way to make these children feel special. The quilting group decided that collectively they could make the hundred or so bunk-bed-sized quilts needed by the time the camp opened the following July. In the meantime, her grandmother, like all the other women in the group, was looking through her old quilts to see if she could find one or two to donate to the camp as wall decorations.

Jennifer felt a chill go up her spine when her grandmother told her about the quilting project. "I knew right away that this was something I wanted to do," she explained. In fact, she instantly knew that this would become part of her life. Her grandmother was delighted when Jennifer asked if she could join the quilting group and sign on to its challenge.

The following August, as the summer camp season was coming to a close, Jennifer, along with her grandmother and all the other women in the quilting group, was invited to attend the annual closing ceremony. There, they were publicly acknowledged and given certificates of appreciation signed by every child who had received a quilt—110 signatures in all.

Finding Meaning: The Antidote to Self-Harm

When Tyler, Lynne, and Jennifer discovered meaningful activities, their self-destructive behavior stopped virtually overnight. In each case, someone in their family, by design or inadvertently, played a role by exposing them to different experiences, and in encouraging them to pursue a new interest. Their new interests gave them an opportunity to see themselves differently, and to feel that they could do something meaningful. For Jennifer, this meant going beyond mere competition with her sister. For Lynne, it meant being able to communicate and bring pleasure to people without having to personally be in the spotlight, and for Tyler it meant finding out that sharing his knowledge was something that others found useful. For all three, doing something meaningful changed their perception of themselves, which allowed them to go from being *nobody* to being *somebody* with something valuable to contribute.

To some it might seem like the solutions to these teens' problems came accidentally. But in truth they were not accidental, so much as they were the result of some adult seeing an opportunity and pursuing it. These opportunities all had one thing in common—they were experiences that allowed these teens to discover something new about themselves. Parents can affect their teens profoundly by keeping their eyes and ears open for such opportunities, and seizing them.

Madonna's song, "Material Girl," claims that we are living in a material world, and that she is a material girl. This is a pretty accurate and also somewhat jaded description of the world in which today's teenagers live. We can't blame Madonna for this reality, for she is only the messenger. In today's world, though, true meaning—the sense that we are here for some purpose other than acquiring and consuming material goods—can be hard to come by. This material world is also intensely competitive, and it promotes jealousy and envy. Teens feel this pressure, at the same time that they are inundated with messages intended to create artificial needs. It is incumbent that you try your best to expose your child to experiences through which he or she might discover a reason for being here other than to acquire and consume as much as possible.

Guiding Your Teen . . . To Overcoming Self-Destructive Behavior

Once again, the point I want to make is that parents need not be helpless bystanders as their teens fall victim to such destructive behaviors as underachievement, combativeness, and self-destructiveness. Here are some guidelines for dealing with the problem of cutting.

FIVE GUIDELINES FOR HELPING YOUR CHILD STOP THE CUTTING

Guideline #1: Recognize that to your teenager, cutting makes sense. Communicating that you understand this is the only way to open communication about a teen's behavior. In contrast, giving them the message that you think your child is crazy is a sure way to cut off communication.

Guideline #2: Don't say, "Don't be shy." This is the statement shy people most dread hearing. From your child's perspective, this is like saying to someone who is short, "Don't be short." Most people recognize that someone can't just will himself or herself to grow; unfortunately, a surprising number of parents act as if they believe that their teenager's temperament can be willed to change. Impatience with teenagers' shyness naturally only makes them feel worse about themselves, whether it comes from you or from others. You may not be able to change how other people react, but you can control your own behavior.

Guideline #3: Sympathize with their shyness and support any efforts to reduce it. This is very different from telling your child not to be that way. Just the act of being sympathetic to the problem of shyness, especially severe shyness, can go a long way toward reducing any self-hatred it may be generating. It can also open the door to a discussion of ways to reduce shyness and the possibility of working with your teenager in role-playing situations in which shyness presents an obstacle to social interaction. This is similar to teaching your teenager to dance. Rather than throwing your child into situation that maximizes self-consciousness and anxiety (like the senior prom), a better way is to practice at home with no one watching. This technique can work with shyness, too, as long as can you avoid coming across as critical or impatient.

Guideline #4: Point out that shy people tend to be sensitive people. Like every cloud, shyness has a silver lining, and you should regularly point out it out. A shy teen's emotional sensitivity and self-consciousness enables many of them to be very empathetic. They can sense what others are feeling, and sometimes even thinking. Shy people can appreciate great art and poetry, and may be talented in these areas themselves. They are also good observers, able to discern nuances in relationships. Gregarious people can have these personal qualities as well, but not to the extent that shy people do.

Guideline #5: Cast a gentle light on the teen growing up in a shadow of an older sibling. Many parents are aware that a younger son or daughter was regularly comparing him- or herself unfavorably to an older sibling, yet are reluctant to bring up the issue for fear of embarrassing their younger child. This is a mistake akin to not talking to your children about drugs or sex for fear of putting such ideas in their heads. Sibling rivalry and competition is as old as Cain and Abel, and you should not hesitate to acknowledge it. It isn't necessary to talk about it every day, any more than you ought to be talking to your kids about sex and drugs every day; on the other hand, it shouldn't be a one-time discussion, either.

It is best to label and talk to your children about sibling rivalry, jealousy, and envy at an early age. That way it becomes "normalized" before it can evolve into something more pathological. If you haven't done that, it's never too late to bring up the issue. Using humor (but not ridicule) can also be helpful when discussing things like jealousy and rivalry. So can sharing personal stories about your own experiences with such things. This allows rivalries to see the light of day, where they can often dissipate.

FAQs

Q: Should I require my teenager to do some community service?

A: Yes, but only if you also do this. Community service that is an integral part of family life—especially if it begins at an early age—is very likely to find its way into a teen's developing identity, and can be a source of inner satisfaction unlike anything that raw competition can create. Meaningfulness is also an antidote to isolation and the feeling that you are a nobody.

You should begin doing this well before your child reaches adolescence. It's a good idea to make some form of community service a family tradition. Here are just a few ideas that can be easily incorporated into family life:

- Help collect toys for needy children at Christmas.

- Collect clothing and other items from friends and neighbors to contribute to a charitable organization.

- Join an organization that provides help and/or entertainment to the elderly or the infirm.

- Help out at a community soup kitchen.

- Contribute bottle and can redemption fees to a charity.

Q: Should I insist that my teenager participate in some group activities like sports or dance?

A: I am not in favor of forcing children or teens to participate in social activities. Rather, bring them along to family activities and gatherings, and let them know you would support such involvement if they chose to pursue it. Lynne's mother, for example, enjoyed taking her places, but did not try to pressure Lynne to commit to anything. If she had taken that approach, Lynne might have opted out of these mother-daughter adventures. Once exposed to it, Lynne became intrigued by the idea of puppetry. Initially, it gave her a way to "socialize" with others without having to do so face-to-face, which was what made her so uncomfortable.

10

using spirituality to build healthy identities

BOOKS ON PARENTING, especially those written by psychologists and other experts on child development, typically do not have much to say about the role of spirituality. In my opinion, this is a serious shortcoming. I think spirituality is not discussed because it is often confused with religion. Although religious people generally would say that they are spiritual, spirituality and religion do not have to go hand in hand, and those who see themselves as spiritual do not necessarily see themselves as religious.

What Is Spirituality?

The bottom line is that spirituality has much more to do with how *we live our lives* than with how *religious we are*. It is entirely possible to be spiritual and religious, but it is also possible to be a spiritual person and not participate in organized religion or even believe in God, at least not in a traditional sense. Native Americans, for example, are highly spiritual people, though their idea of a "higher power" is much different from the idea of God as taught in modern monotheistic religions.

In addition, people sometimes confuse spirituality with other-worldliness. In their minds, a "spiritual" person is someone who prays a lot, is completely self-sacrificing, or foregoes physical comforts in favor of getting in touch with God. However, this is not what I mean when I talk about spirituality and why it is important to your child's identity development.

In working with teens, I try to show them the differences between what I call a *spiritual lifestyle* and a *nonspiritual lifestyle*.

SPIRITUAL LIFESTYLE	NONSPIRITUAL LIFESTYLE
• Concerned with *meaning:* Asks, "Why am I here?"	• Concerned with accumulating *things:* Asks, "What do I want?"
• Identifies with *relationships:* Measures success by the quality of important relationships.	• Identifies with *status:* Measures success through name-brand clothing, job title, etc.
• Believes in *interdependency:* Reaching out to others and helping others is vital to a successful life.	• Believes in *self-sufficiency:* We can do everything by ourselves and need no help from others.
• Is *charitable* and *generous*.	• Is inclined to *hoard* and be *stingy*.
• Is *grateful* for what she or he has.	• Is *envious* and *self-pitying*.

Reality Check: Bye-Bye Bob (the Dad) and Ingrate Emily (the Teen)

Bob was highly successful, but was living a nonspiritual lifestyle, and paying the price for it. Bob was a senior vice-president in charge of strategic planning for a major corporation. He had a keen intelligence, exceptional social skills, and he had risen through the ranks based on his talent and drive. He was divorced, and ever since his ex-wife's death in a car accident three years earlier, he had custody of his daughter, Emily, who was now eighteen and a freshman in college.

Bob had what he called a "decent" relationship with Emily for the several years prior to her mother's death. He saw her weekly, except when he was traveling on business, which was usually two or three times a month. She also visited him overnight, but this had become less frequent the older she got, which meant it happened about once every five or six weeks. The overwhelming majority of Bob's time, though, was taken up with work. An average workweek for him was sixty hours or more. He worked in the office; he worked on airplanes; he worked from home. Weekends were not much different from weekdays. He traveled a lot for the company, including a good deal of foreign travel, which ate up much more time than domestic travel. From the first day that Emily moved in with him, Bob felt that their relationship had deteriorated steadily. He believed that Emily did not respect him, or appreciate the material advantages that his success brought her. "She doesn't lack for anything," Bob explained. "Emily doesn't seem to realize that. She doesn't seem the least bit interested in what I do, or recognize how my success and hard work have made her life easier. And she never says 'thank you' for anything."

> **HEADS UP!** *Just be Mom or Dad.*

Some parents, like Bob, expect their kids to love them because of the money they make, or the position they hold. Your children may respect what you do for a living, but, in the end, this respect is based on the quality of your relationship with them, not the position you hold somewhere else. Others may call us "boss" or "doctor," or even "Your Royal Highness," but to your child you will always be, first and foremost, simply Dad or Mom. It's a mistake to think that your family will be organized like your workplace—that you can be the boss in both places—or that your child's esteem for you will be based on the title you have or the position you hold. If you feel disappointed that your teenager doesn't appreciate your success, you'd be wise to examine your relationship.

Emily perceived that her father was living a very nonspiritual lifestyle (although she hadn't put that label on it), and she was reacting to it. Emily was not innately ungrateful; neither was she spoiled. Her mother had provided for her, but there had always been priorities, and sacrifices had to be made. She recognized the material things her father provided; at the same time, she found it hard to feel "proud" of him simply because he was successful. What had always struck her more than his success was his relative absence from her life.

Emily's rebellion against her father took the form of deliberate indifference to anything remotely connected to the business world. She was doing well in college, but had not declared a major. When she told her father that she was leaning toward in psychology, he moaned and rolled his eyes. He told Emily that the only way she could hope to make a living as a psychologist was to stay in school until she got a doctorate, which, as far as he was concerned, was a waste of time. He had never been to a counselor in his life—not for marriage counseling, and not after his ex-wife's death—and he made it clear that he could not imagine ever doing so.

Bob was very proud of his position in the company. He was also proud that he owned two expensive cars and a luxury condominium, as well as time shares in both Santa Fe and Aruba. He denied himself little. He exercised regularly, and he ate well, although his alcohol consumption had increased over the past few years, and he'd recently been diagnosed with hypertension.

I consider Bob's lifestyle nonspiritual, because he was much more concerned with what he had and with his social status than with any purpose his life might have outside of these things. He confused his identity with what he did and what he owned. He believed that he could be an island unto himself; he devoted relatively little time to his relationship with Emily (or anyone else) and gave virtually none of his money or time to any charitable causes. He was aware of the lack of real closeness between him and Emily, but attributed this to her. He was wrong.

The fact that Emily had a functional, resilient identity was due mostly to her relationship with her mother, which was more or less already formed by the time she came to live with her father. Despite being able to offer Emily fewer material advantages, her mother had been a better model of spirituality. (This is also why some children who are raised in poverty become criminals, while others become successful and happy people.)

HEADS UP! *How balanced are you?*

Take some time to reflect on your own lifestyle, with an eye toward seeing how well it meets the criteria for being spiritual or nonspiritual. Keep in mind as you do that many people fall somewhere in the middle. Although a few people may be extraordinarily charitable and generous, many more fall somewhere in between generous and stinginess. On the other hand, exceptional stinginess and hoarding are clear signs of a nonspiritual lifestyle. It boils down to *balance:* balancing any desire for material things with some desire to help others, and balancing a desire to do things for yourself with a willingness to reach out to others.

The Effect of Spirituality on Identity

As your adolescent views the world around and seeks to carve out a sense of who she or he is and the meaning of life, it is inevitable that they are influenced not so much by the things that you tell them, as by the example you set. Take a moment to think back on your own adolescence; I believe you will see that this was true for you as well. It is easy to sometimes fall into the trap of believing that what you say has more weight than what you do. Nothing could be further from the truth.

No parent is a perfect model of spiritual living. I'm certainly not, and I don't know anyone who is. On the other hand, if we hope to guide our children toward healthy identities, then you must strive to achieve some *balance* between spiritual and nonspiritual living in our own lives. This can be a challenge today. It seems impossible, for example, for people—adults as well as children and teens—to become immune to the influence of marketing and advertising. I've no doubt that we all are driven in part by "needs" that have been created for us by the media: the need for a global positioning system in our car, for a cell phone that takes pictures, or for an MP3 player that can download movies. Yet, if we allow ourselves to be swept away by advertising, then we can hardly expect our children to be different.

Reality Check: All-About-Me Amber

Amber was an attractive seventeen-year-old whose parents, Ben and Hillary, felt they had effectively lost control of their daughter.

Despite her pretty features (and great hair), Amber appeared harsh, mainly because she rarely smiled. A subtle frown was what her face seemed to settle into whenever she wasn't talking. She was also spoiled rotten. It began when she was an infant. Her parents believed that it was good to give her everything she wanted, not realizing that by doing so they failed to establish appropriate limits. As a result, Amber grew up feeling that she was not just an important *part* of the universe, but also the *center* of it.

Amber was not only spoiled, but also careless. At seventeen, she'd already totaled two cars and her insurance premiums—paid by her folks—were outrageous. When Ben offered to buy Amber a third car—this time a used one—she threw a fit, insisting that she wanted a new car. This attitude carried over to everything else that Amber had, including clothes and jewelry, which she rarely took care of, and was forever misplacing.

As you may have surmised, Ben and Hillary were inclined to live their own lives that same way. They, too, often spent money they didn't have, only to end up having to climb out of debt. Fortunately, Ben had been able to do that. They could not deny themselves things they perceived as "needs," which included tropical vacations and expensive status cars. Ben was the son of a hardworking couple and was raised in a middle-class community, but his parents acted as if they were poor. Ben recalled that they always complained about not having enough money, and, when he was young, he had few of the things—clothing, toys, etc.—that most of his contemporaries enjoyed.

He grew up feeling like a have-not, which could have contributed to his desire for material things, but in addition, Ben's parents were not particularly spiritual. They were often envious of others. His father often complained that he "hadn't gotten a fair shake" in life, that he had "gotten the short end of the stick," while his older brother (Ben's uncle), who had excelled in school and gone on to become an attorney, "had all the breaks."

Ben's mother, who was also quick to find fault with others, was openly resentful of those who had more than she did, and was openly sorry that she hadn't had an easier life. This tendency toward self-pity in Ben's parents runs counter to the gratitude that is one hallmark of a spiritual person, and it seems to have fueled Ben's craving for material comforts. Indeed, like Bob, he was inclined to confuse who he was with what he had.

Last, Amber's family life lacked structure. They had never been interested in or become involved in any religious activity; nor had they ever consistently observed any holidays. They were as apt to take Amber to a restaurant or a movie on Thanksgiving as to cook and share a family meal. Christmas was little more than a marathon of gift opening. There were virtually no day-to-day rituals that were observed as Amber was growing up. Although Hillary cooked, the family rarely shared meals. Amber ate early by herself, and then went off to watch television or call friends. Ben and Hillary ate dinner later on while watching the news on television.

When Amber stopped going to school in the middle of her junior year and announced her intention to drop out because "It's just too boring," Ben and Hillary panicked. Instead, Amber decided to pursue a GED (a general equivalency diploma) through a program that required her to take classes two evenings a week plus one Saturday a month. This was as much schooling as she could bear.

When her parents tried to argue, explaining that a high school diploma was more valuable than a GED, Amber fought back ferociously, as she always did when she was frustrated. She pointed out that her father, who owned his own successful business, had also dropped out of high school; she ignored the fact that her father still worked fifty hours a week, and had devoted himself to his business ever since he'd started it.

TOO LITTLE, TOO LATE

Unfortunately, at this point there was little that Ben and Hillary could do. As optimistic as I am, it really was too late for Ben and Hillary to start setting limits or begin modeling a spiritual lifestyle. Instead, something would have to happen in Amber's life that would cause her to see things from a different perspective. Amber's identity, which could be summed up in one word—*entitled*—was already established.

This could happen to your child—if you fail to set limits (the earlier the better), if you fail to build a bond between you through family rituals and traditions, and if you fail to lead even a modestly spiritual lifestyle.

Guiding Your Teen . . . To a Balanced Life

Here are the guidelines I recommend that you follow in order to instill a measure of spirituality into your family life. This spirituality, in turn, will help ensure that the identity your child develops is one that will lead them to happiness in work and love:

SIX GUIDELINES FOR CREATING A SPIRITUAL LIFESTYLE

Guideline #1: Ask yourself not only "What do I want?" but also "Why am I here?" These are important questions that you should ask your children, but before you can do this effectively, you need to ask yourself the same questions. In fact, you need to ask yourself these questions more than once. This dynamic between what I want and why I am here should become a conscious theme, which, in turn, can become the subject of an ongoing dialogue between you and your teenager. When you have this dialogue, it is important to remember that wanting things is not in any way abnormal. Rather, the point of this dialogue is to instill a sense of the need for *balance* in your and your adolescent's lives. It also helps to make you more transparent as a parent (see Chapter 4).

A life dominated by the question, "What do I want?" will be a life that rarely knows contentment. It is easy enough these days to be seduced into such a lifestyle, but, as a rule, any satisfaction we experience simply from getting the thing we want quickly disappears as we focus on the thing we want *next*.

Balanced against consumerism is *meaning*. Life is about more than acquiring and consuming things, but also about doing something. To remind yourself of this, you might find it helpful to tell yourself, each day, something like, "Before I was born, God knew my name," or "I am here for a purpose."

If you believe that life has meaning and purpose, your actions will communicate this to your child, and purpose will become an integral part of your teen's identity. That purpose may be different from the purpose you see for your child's life, but it will be a purpose nonetheless. Some examples of activities that give a sense of meaning and purpose to one's life are:

- Helping those less fortunate than you

- Introducing art, music, and other forms of creativity into people's lives

- Raising a child responsibly

- Helping to preserve the earth and its natural resources

- Making people laugh

- Teaching the illiterate how to read

- Doing charitable work

Guideline #2: Focus on your relationships, not your status. Don't let yourself fall into the trap that Bob did; that is, don't assume that your child will respect and be proud of you because of the position you hold or the mount of money you make. If your child is proud of you for these things, it will be the icing on the cake; the cake itself is the quality of your relationship. There's been much talk about spending "quality time" with children, meaning time one-on-one, or time spent doing special things together, such as going to a museum. The idea was that a small amount of "quality time" could make up for not spending a lot of time together, or for spending time together but not necessarily interacting one-on-one or doing special things.

In theory, "quality time" sounds fine. However, in practice, it is rarely a substitute for time spent just interacting with one another. In fact, trying to substitute "quality time" (in the sense of doing special things), for time spent interacting with your teenager can lead to spoiling him or her instead of building your relationship. Dr. Phil McGraw once commented that some of the most meaningful time he spent with his two sons was just shooting hoops in their driveway. This is a perfect example of how important time spent interacting can be.

Some ways to increase the amount of interaction that you and your teen have include:

- Cooking a meal together

- Cleaning a room together

- Planning meals for the weekend and then food shopping together

- Shooting hoops

- Taking a hike

- Walking the dog together after dinner

- Going to a movie and talking about it afterward

- Browsing through a bookstore

- Going to a gallery opening and looking at art while sampling the cheese

The possibilities for spending time together doing something ordinary are literally limitless. The rule is, *whatever you do, think about doing it together.* This will do more to increase the esteem in which you are held by your child than what you do or how much you make.

Guideline #3: Don't try to be "the captain of your ship, the master of your fate," all by yourself. Here, I am talking about humility, meaning that it's important to recognize some limits in what you can achieve through individual willpower alone. It also means that you should not see yourself as an island, but as an integral part of a larger group: marriage, family, community, etc. Traditionally, Americans have believed strongly in personal willpower; for example, the adage that any child can grow up to be president. This is fine as long as it does not lead to arrogance or the idea that you should never need any help with anything.

For this reason, it is important that you teach and model humility. If you don't, then your child's identity may contain elements of entitlement, even grandiosity. Such an identity may be functional in that it can lead to ambition and drive, but it is not very functional when it comes to marriage and family life. In addition, people who are arrogant and entitled tend to give up or become angry or depressed when things don't go their way.

Here are some ideas for teaching and modeling humility:

- *Take stock of your own beliefs.* Can you acknowledge that you sometimes need help? Do believe in the importance of people relying on each other, as in a marriage or family, or do you believe people should do everything by and for themselves? Do you believe that there are times when we need to reach out to others to accomplish our goals?

- *Practice offering and asking for help.* Within your marriage and in your day-to-day relationship with your child, make a point of offering help, and also of asking for help on occasion. For example, get a puzzle and ask your child to help you with it or ask your teenager for his or her opinion about something. You'd be surprised at how well teenagers can respond to a request for help or an opinion. Not only will this make your teenager feel that she or he has something to offer, but also it models humility, which is something you'd like your child to incorporate into her or his identity as it develops.

- *Give prayer a chance.* If you believe in prayer, you will not find this difficult. Regardless of your personal beliefs, I encourage you to be open to your child believing in God or some "higher power," and even to praying. I know many parents who personally have doubts about God, but who join their children in saying a bedtime prayer. As for adolescents, I recommend that parents be public about anything they do that might resemble prayer. For example, if you begin your day with a meditation, try doing this in a place in your home where your teenager can observe you doing it.

Guideline #4: Learn to apologize. It is as important for healthy adolescent identity development that parents be able to admit when they are wrong or make a mistake, as it is for them to set and enforce reasonable limits. Both will help your child and teenager appreciate the fact that just as there are boundaries in life, it is also true that no one is perfect, and that everyone makes mistakes. Without boundaries, and without humility, the identity that emerges during adolescence is likely to be distorted. It's one thing for you your teenager to feel *effective*; it's another thing entirely for your adolescent to feel *omnipotent and perfect.*

The simplest way to set this example is to learn to say "I'm sorry," for example, after:

- Inadvertently saying or doing something that hurts your child's feelings

- Wrongly accusing your teenager of having done something wrong or having violated a limit

- Venting your frustration over something else on your child

- Criticizing your child for failing to meet an unreasonable expectation

- Forgetting to do something you had promised to do

You'd be surprised to know how great an impact a simple apology from a parent can have on a teenager.

Guideline #5: Express gratitude often. The longstanding Christian tradition of saying grace before meals is a ritual that allows a family to express gratitude publicly and together on a daily basis. However, there are an infinite number of variations on how gratitude can be expressed. Grace can evoke God; alternatively, it can be a simple expression of thanks for being together and enjoying the fruits of the family's common labor. This little ritual, short and simple as it is, strenghtens the family bond.

I encourage you to incorporate some form of ritual whenever your family sits down together to share a meal. In some families, the responsibility for the prayer or statement of thanks is rotated among parents and children; in other families, it is done by the parents. Some parents use a short meditation instead of a prayer. However, you choose to do it, just be sure that it is a statement of gratitude or thanks for what you have.

The ability to express gratitude is a strong asset in life, and if your teenager is able to incorporate this into her or his emerging identity, she or he will be better off for it. Saying grace or expressing gratitude at meal times is a convenient way to incorporate gratitude into family life, but it is by no means the only way. True gratitude shines through in a way that everyone can see.

If you would like your teen to incorporate the capacity for gratitude into his or her identity, then you would be wise to express gratitude yourself, openly and regularly. Try making simple statements like those listed below. If you find this uncomfortable at first, it may be that you just aren't used to being grateful. It should get easier with practice.

- "What a beautiful day!"

- "Boy, but it's good to be alive!"

- "I'm grateful that you're my child."

- "I'm so glad I'm feeling well today."

- "Sometimes when I look around me at other people's situations, I'm grateful for what I have."

Guideline #6: Be charitable. Learning the value of charitable work is another antidote to egocentrism and selfishness. Once again, if you want your teenager to incorporate an interest in charity as part of her or his emerging sense of self, you need to *show* this through your own actions.

Most people, when they think about charity, think first about donating *money;* for example, contributing regularly to their church, synagogue, or mosque, or to the United Way campaign, or sponsoring an underprivileged child in another country, and so on. While these are all worthwhile charities, in terms of developing your child's identity, it is charitable *work* that makes the greatest impression. The very best scenario is one where you and your teen participate together in some charitable work.

Here are a few options. I know you can think of many more:

- Helping to cook and serve a meal at a local community soup kitchen twice a year

- Collecting and delivering deposit bottles for the local high school annual charity drive

- Volunteering to do light maintenance work at your house of worship

- Collecting and delivering Toys for Tots during the holiday season

Shared charity work, even if it happens only occasionally, will help your teen see him- or herself as a valuable part of a whole: The family and community. At the same time, it generates a feel of effectiveness. As it evolves, your child's sense of self is more likely to include an element of being a part of a whole when he or she is exposed to such experiences. It also gives a teenager some perspective on how fortunate he or she is. Through charitable work, your adolescent can see firsthand that it is possible to survive tough times, or achieve goals, by learning to rely on others and work cooperatively.

In contrast, doing nothing for others promotes a teen's perception that he or she is the center of the universe. An identity that is built around that idea is apt to be *fragile*, leaving your teen vulnerable to depression and anxiety as an adult.

FAQs

Q: Should I let my teenager watch television, since that is likely to lead to false "needs"?

A: Some writers see the media as the cause of much adolescent misery from depression to substance abuse to underachievement, and advocate that children not be allowed to watch. I don't agree. It doesn't make sense to try to insulate your child or teenager from the world. Even if you could, at some point your child is going to be exposed to it. Rather than trying to insulate kids from the world, I'm an advocate of *inoculating* them against some of its more dangerous aspects. A healthy identity—one that includes elements of spirituality—is better insurance for a happy and productive life than any amount of shielding you can do.

Q: I stopped participating in the religion I was raised in many years ago and I have no interest in returning. Does that mean I'm harming my teenager?

A: Not necessarily. I believe that spirituality has more to do with lifestyle than religious activity. If you follow a spiritual lifestyle, you will expose your child to spiritual values, which your teenager can incorporate into his or her identity. I also recommend that you allow your child to explore participation in organized religion if he or she shows an interest in doing so.

Q: I want my teenager to grow into an adult who is self-confident and believes in himself. Isn't it contradictory for

me to be telling him that he should be relying on others?

A: There is no inherent conflict between self-confidence and humility. The best way to help build a child's self-confidence (what psychologists today refer to as "self-efficacy") is through success. Exposing your child to challenges where he or she can experience success is one way to do this. Actually, children and teens do this with little or no encouragement. Encouraging your child or teen to take on challenges is fine; however, pushing your child or teen to go far beyond the level of challenge he or she would choose for him- or herself may not be such a good idea.

Believing that you are not an island unto yourself should not be confused with a lack of self-confidence. Neither will modeling such a belief nor expressing it to your teenager lead him or her to become overly dependent on others. On the contrary, your child will become stronger when he or she recognizes both his or her own abilities *and* the need to work with others, when he or she acknowledges the need for help at times. Ask any good baseball, basketball, football, or soccer coach, and you'll hear the same thing.

APPENDIX:
Fast FAQs Guide to Parenting Teens

Most parents (myself included) at one time or another have probably said in despair, "They never gave me a manual!" Well, here it is! This Fast FAQs Guide summarizes the key elements in the preceding ten chapters and provides you with a convenient reference for handling difficult situations and for helping to promote healthy identity development in your teenager. I suggest you keep the book in a convenient place so the guide will be easy to grab when you need it.

The Fast FAQs Guide follows the same organization as the chapters in the book, presented here in question-and-answer format. Find the issue you want some help with and then read that section. You may find it useful at times to reread one or more chapters for a more in-depth view.

You can use it when you are faced with a particular situation and are unsure what to do. Glancing through the questions, you should come upon one or two that are relevant to what you're dealing with. Another way to use the guide is to read one question every week, and think about (even better, talk about) how it may apply to your teenager. In whatever way you use the guide, I hope you find it useful not just today, but through your years as a parent.

What is identity?

Identity refers to our inner sense of who we are and why we are here. Identity includes your values (what you stand for), your goals, and your sense of where you fit into the scheme of things: who you care for and who cares for you, where you belong, what your talents, tastes and preferences are, and so on. Settling on an identity is the major developmental outcome of adolescence. The more hardened your identity becomes, the more difficult it is to change it. What is commonly referred to as an "epiphany" is an experience that leads an adult to alter his or her identity.

Where does identity come from?

The psychologist Erik Erikson, who first wrote about developing identity and named it as the main psychological task of adolescence, believed that teens begin the process of identity development by seeking out *people and ideas to believe in.* I believe this process begins earlier than adolescence, but that it is not until a child has the intellectual capacity to think critically that they can truly begin to assess who their heroes are and what they believe in and stand for. Children tend to hold uncritical, one-dimensional views of their parents (typically as all good and all-knowing), but teens see things more three-dimensionally. In today's world, other factors such as the powerful adolescent subculture and the media strongly influence the process of how teens decides who they are.

How does identity relate to behavior?

Behavior is the outward manifestation of identity. Thus, your sense of *who you are* strongly influences *what you do.* It is the lens through which you see the world—and the way you see the world has a strong influence on how you behave and what you believe. If you see the world as a threatening place and think of yourself as the toughest dude on the block, then your behavior will reflect that identity and will be very different than it would be if you thought of yourself as a peacemaker. If you think of yourself as defective and vulnerable, you will behave differently than you would if you thought of yourself as competent and resilient.

Do rewards and punishments influence behavior, or just identity?
Rewards and punishments influence behavior, but they are more effective with children than teenagers. If you frequently turn to rewards and punishments in order to control your teen's behavior, you will find it less and less effective. Especially with punishment, *less is more:* The less you use it, the more effective it is.

What does my son's behavior say about his identity?
Your son's behavior is actually a window onto his sense of who he is and where he is going. Chronic aggressive behavior, for example, suggests your adolescent sees the world as a dangerous place and may be moving toward an identity that adopts a survival of the fittest view as a life goal. In contrast, an overly cautious approach to life suggests that your teen sees himself as defective (incompetent) and fragile. An inability to take no for an answer or delay gratification suggests an inflated identity (being the center of the universe). And so on.

How does a teen's identity begin to form?
As the character Eliza in the play *Pygmalion* aptly put it: "The difference between a flower girl and a lady is not how she acts, but how she is treated." The lesson you should take from this is: *The way you treat your child will play a dominant role in the identity that emerges during adolescence.* If you treat your child as fragile and incompetent, your teenager may very well come to believe it and act accordingly. If you relate to your child as someone who is not just loved and valued, but the very center of the universe, the teenager may very well embrace an inflated sense of self. Conversely, the earlier you begin to treat your daughter like a lady or your son like a gentleman, the sooner your child is will begin thinking that way.

How can I get a sense of what identity my teenage daughter might be developing?

First, you need to remember what your identity was like when you were a teenager, so that you don't make the mistake of trying to shape your teen's identity to mirror your own. Exercise 1–1 on page 6 can help you to do this. Second, make sure you spend more time listening to your teen than offering advice or telling her what to do. The more you are able to listen, the clearer the picture will be of who your teen thinks she is.

Can a family crisis—for example, if I lose my job or undergo treatment for cancer—have traumatic effects on my teenage son's identity?

There is a false assumption that family crises are necessarily traumatic for children and teens. In fact, whether or not a crisis or trauma has a lasting negative effect has a lot to do with your son's identity—with how he views himself, and what he expects life to be like. If your teen sees himself as capable and resilient, and understands that life will include occasional crises and challenges, the issue becomes what he can *learn* from a crisis, not how much it can *damage* him. For this reason, the experience of coping successfully with crises builds a resilient identity. Your goal is not to insulate your child from all adversity, but to show your child how to manage adversity.

What should I do if my teenager daughter begins to express feelings of hopelessness about the future?

The belief that negative experiences leave permanent effects can have devastating effects on a teen's identity and therefore how that child behaves. That kind of pessimism sets the stage for alienation and depression. It is vital that you communicate two things: First, that the past does not determine the future; second, that no matter what may have gone before, your child still has choices to make about what the future will be. Of course, you should sympathize with the pain your daughter may have experienced or with her frustrations, but you must never go along with the idea that pain or frustration is grounds for hopelessness.

How does making decisions foster a healthy identity?

The very act of making a decision promotes the idea that your child has *choices*. Beginning as early as possible, parents should set limits and then encourage children to make decisions within those limits. For example, toddlers can be taken to a store and asked to choose between two pairs of pants. When your children begin kindergarten, they can be allowed to choose among three or four different backpacks. You can also give your children some choice about the clothes they would like to wear to school the next day. And so on. Doing this accomplishes two things: It introduces the idea of choice, while also introducing the concept of limits. By the time your children reaches adolescence, they will have long records of accomplishment in making decisions, and will possess a belief in the power of choice.

What should I do if my teenager acts as if she believes she is an outsider and has no close friends?

First acknowledge the way your child feels, but don't try to immediately change it. Don't try to force your daughter to socialize when she doesn't want to, for that will only increase her sense of alienation. Make it acceptable to not fit in; take the position that she may just be one of those "individuals" who needs time to find the right niche. Point out as often as you can that many creative people don't necessarily "fit the mold." Point out the ways in which your daughter is an individual. You may need to do some searching, but if you are comfortable with the idea that many happy and successful people are also nonconformists, you may open the way for your teenager to feel proud of who she is, instead of angry and alienated. If your child begins to feel okay about the idea of being an individual, eventually your daughter may gravitate toward other individuals.

Is it okay to tell my teen that he cannot associate with certain people?

Absolutely! Part of your parental responsibility is to set reasonable limits. You also need to set limits with respect to attire, curfews, use of the phone and computer, and so on. Within those limits, however, you need to encourage your teenager to make choices. It may be tempting to blame bad behavior on the influence of a bad peer group. However, if you see your teenager drifting toward a group of peers you regard as a potential negative influence, it may also be a sign that he is moving toward an unhealthy identity. Take this as a warning sign, and using the techniques presented throughout this book, steer your teen in another direction.

Is it okay to talk about my personal struggles with my teenagers?

Yes, definitely, but such conversations need to be *balanced* with talks about positive aspects of your own life. I once spoke with a teen who told me how her parents came home every day and complained about how much they hated their jobs. They never spoke about any accomplishments, only about how awful management and their working conditions were, and how badly underpaid they were. Seeing themselves as helpless victims in this way only promoted a similar identity in their two teenage children, neither of whom was motivated to work hard in school. In contrast, sharing stories about overcoming adversity, and even stories about how you came to make difficult decisions, will encourage your teens to incorporate a similar attitude in their own emerging identity.

My son used to look up to me, but since he turned fourteen, he acts as if I've lost 50 IQ points. He makes faces at everything I say, and picks arguments with me all the time. What's going on, and what do I do?

Get used to it. Your son has become an adolescent. Don't confuse his argumentativeness with any loss of love or respect for you. On the contrary, if he truly did not respect you he would not even bother to argue with you. Keep in mind that arguing is also the way we train men and women to become lawyers. The method is called *dialectics*. It involves first arguing a position, then arguing for the opposite position, and then going back and forth until consensus is reached. It can be difficult to see it this way, but that is in fact what is going on. Giving in to your son's argument would be wrong, just as never seeking a middle ground (consensus) is the wrong thing to do. Engage your teen in the dialectic process, keeping in mind that the result of a healthy dialectic will be a healthy identity for your teen.

My teenage daughter tests virtually every limit I set and wants to talk it to death. I want to keep communication between us open, but I don't want to argue until the cows come home every day. What's your advice?

To begin with, let your teen know that you recognize and respect her right to disagree, as well as the need for her to make more decisions for herself as she matures. Don't ridicule her in any way. Saying "Because I said so" is not a good approach either. It only invites rebellion, and it doesn't help a teen learn to make decisions. Point out decisions that you do allow your daughter to make. Of course, there needs to be a limit to just how long you allow an argument to go on. If you allow it to go on too long, your teen may succeed in getting you to lose your temper. Some parents find it helpful to use a legal analogy: Just as every lawyer gets a chance to present an argument before a judge, at some point the time for arguing is over and a decision is made. The way to end the debate is to say, "Okay, I've heard you out, but I haven't changed my mind. So the answer is no."

Why has my sweet little daughter turned into a shrew? How can I communicate with her?

The answer to this question is the same as the answer to the last one: your daughter has moved from one developmental stage (childhood) to another (adolescence). She is trying to define herself. At this point mothers in particular find that their relationship with their teenage daughter has become contentious. The process of forming an identity can lead to outright defiance and oppositional behavior. Daughters may test the limits in terms of clothing and make-up, as well as where they can go and how accountable they must be. In some ways, open mother-daughter conflict has an advantage; you know what you are dealing with. Daughters who may appear to be conforming on the outside may actually be exploring their individuality in secret by getting into drugs or engaging in risky sexual behavior, for example. As I have advised throughout this book, engage in a dialogue. And that mostly means learning to listen—not necessarily agree, but listen.

May I express any expectations for my teenaged son? What's the best way to do this?

Yes, you are entitled to express your expectations. You want your teen to grow to be a happy and successful adult. If you perceive that your son has talents, you want him to realize his potential. The thing to watch out for is whether your teen is living *his* life, or some life that *you* have designed. Regularly ask yourself this question: When my teenager is thirty, do I want her to look back and realize that he or she is living a life I designed, or a life that he designed? "Hothouse" kids (see Chapter 5) are those who, if they give in to their parents' expectations, are likely to wake up one day and realize that they haven't been living their own lives. It may actually be healthier for teens to rebel against being treated like a rare flower. If you've ever spoken with an adult who gave in to parental expectations and tried to be the person their parents wanted them to be, instead of forming their own identity and living their own lives, you know that they can be very depressed. Strive to be a parent who wants his or her son to succeed, but who also allows him to chart his own course in life.

What's the best way to proceed with teenagers who tends to give up easily and have low expectations for what they can accomplish?

These are signs of a fragile identity in progress. It's obvious what kind of adult life these attitudes are likely to lead to. You can pursue several strategies. First, in conversations you can frequently bring up the idea that everyone possesses both limitations and strengths, and consistently point out your children's real strengths. These can include strengths that reflect on character, such as honesty, generosity, and the capacity to show love, just as much as they can be intellectual, athletic, or artistic abilities. Point out that our society may place too much emphasis on the latter, and not enough on strength of character. Second, you can expose your teens to a variety of experiences that could pique their interest and lead to successful experiences. Again, society places a premium on intellectual and athletic abilities, but music, art, writing, and even hobbies may represent uncharted waters in which to discover untapped interests and talents. Third, give some thought to whether your children, for one reason or another, are in the process of developing an underentitled identity, thinking that they don't deserve or just should not expect to get much of what they want. This feeling may not be of their making, however. You would be wise to take a look at such things as how many choices and decisions you have typically allowed them to make, and whether this warrants some change on your part.

My teenager acts as if he ought to get everything he wants and he throws a fit when he can't. How should I deal with this?

These are signs that an *over*entitled identity is in the making. The person with a healthy identity believes that he or she is truly a valued part of the universe. The overentitled person, however, views him or herself as the *center* of the universe, a person who should never be denied anything. If you fail to set reasonable limits, you risk promoting an overentitled identity in your teen, and changing that can be a mighty challenge. Teens do not give up such attitudes easily, and they are formulas for disaster, because few but their parents are likely to play into such expectations. Ironically, the person who is overentitled may also be a person who gives up easily, since he or she does not expect to have to work hard to get something, or persevere in the face of adversity. To reverse this, you first need to revisit the limits you've set, and probably make them more reasonable. Then you need to find the courage and stamina to go toe-to-toe with your teen in enforcing a more realistic view of the world and your teen's place in it.

What does it mean when my teen gets all upset over the littlest frustration, or when things don't go exactly as she had planned? How should I react?

These behaviors are signs that your teen is moving toward a *fragile* identity. The first thing you need to do is to check whether you have this same attitude. Do you tend to get upset over little, unexpected changes in your routine or plans? Do people say you are "thin-skinned"? If not, good. On the other hand, if this describes you, then your teen may simply be incorporating this part of your identity into hers. An identity that includes this attitude makes a person vulnerable to chronic anxiety. Try a different attitude on for size. John Lennon put it well when he wrote, "Life is what happens to you while you're making plans." In other words, life is full of surprises, and we shouldn't expect it to be otherwise. If you try this, you may find yourself becoming more even-keeled, less thrown off by minor frustrations. If you adopt this attitude, you put yourself in a better position to talk credibly to your daughter whenever she overreacts.

It's difficult for me to stand by and watch my teenager struggle. How do I resist the urge to step in?

Think back to when your teen was just a toddler of, say, four years old. Remember how often he or she said to you, "Let me do it!"

when you were about to pour a glass of milk, open a bag of cookies, or pour batter onto the griddle to make a pancake. Can you remember how your child challenged him- or herself physically and mentally when trying to climb things, put a puzzle together, or draw a picture? Facing adversity in this way is how children grow and develop self-confidence. It is the foundation of a resilient identity. The same process continues in adolescence. Teens need to be encouraged to challenge themselves, and you can help by making it clear that you respect the *process* of challenging yourself, regardless of the *outcome*. Practice saying, "Go for it!" as often as you can, and celebrate the effort as much as the results.

My son is interested only in sports but is unmotivated in school. His grades are not high enough for him to qualify. Wouldn't it be better for him to play than not play?

I'm sure your son would enjoy playing, but think about the implications to him if you were to intervene and try to change the rules to make an exception for him. A better alternative is to respect the rules and communicate your confidence that your son can improve his grades. Ask regularly if there is anything you can do to help him academically. If you can afford it, offer to pay for a tutor. Keep in mind, though, that almost every high school offers free tutoring and teachers want nothing more than for a teenager to succeed.

What's the best way to inject a spirit of adventure into my son's developing identity?

The best way by far is to do it together. Depending on your own experiences, this may be more or less easy to do. Even parents whose own parents never offered or encouraged adventure can find ways to develop this in themselves and promote it in their teenager. Organizations such as the Appalachian Mountain Club offer supervised adventure experiences where parent and teen can explore nature and learn new skills. Another approach is to learn something together, such as cross-country or downhill skiing, surfing, or wind sailing. Finally, learning to explore the world together, for example, through trips sponsored by the Audubon Society, can be exciting. All of these things will help guide your teen toward a healthy, resilient identity. One family said that a five-day river trip through the Grand Canyon brought them together and boosted their self-confidence as nothing they'd ever experienced had before.

How much time should I allow my teen to watch television or spend on the Internet?

It isn't only how much time, but whether your teen has unrestricted, unsupervised access to the Internet, and whether you have established any limits not only on what your child can watch on television but what kind of music your teen can buy or download. Ideally, you will have begun this well before adolescence. The Internet carries many risks, most of which are no more than two or three clicks away. Music can be benign, but it can also be morbid and violent. Television does not always present parents in a positive light.

Keep in mind your child is seeking "ideas and people to believe in" as he or she seeks to carve out an identity. Your child's values, expectations for the future, and beliefs about relationships are all aspects of identity. These things are too precious to simply leave unattended. Although I do not believe in forbidding children to watch television, listen to music, or experience the Internet, don't hesitate to talk about the potential dangers and negative messages inherent in each and to monitor your child's access to them, just as you would educate your child about the dangers of knives and monitor his or her access to them. Feel free to discuss music lyrics and the scripts of television shows. As teens get older, they will inevitably have to make more choices in what they watch and what they listen to, but having a parent-teen dialogue as a context for these decisions can go a long way toward minimizing any deleterious effects these integral aspects of modern life can have on identity development.

How will rituals and traditions help me set limits as a parent?
Parents of young children have a lot more leverage when it comes to controlling behavior than they do by the time their kids become adolescents. Any parent of a teen will vouch for this. Your influence is rooted much more in the *bond* between you and your child than it is in any reward or punishment you can dole out. When the parent-teen bond is strong, approval and disapproval are more powerful than reward and punishment. In addition, when the bond is strong, discussion becomes a powerful way to resolve differences.

There are many ways to build this bond between you and your teen, such as sharing challenges and adventures. Another powerful tool for connecting is through family rituals and traditions. Changes in our society, most of which are economically driven, have made maintaining rituals and traditions a challenge for many parents. However, it is absolutely vital that they be maintained.

If you have drifted away from organized religion and the rituals and traditions that can be found there, you need to be creative and invent your own. If your teen has grown up without many rituals and traditions, you may encounter resistance when you try to introduce them. Your teen's attitude may be that it's silly. One way to deal with such resistance is to make any rituals and traditions you settle on fun for all involved. Going to a restaurant that everyone likes, seeing a movie that everyone wants to see, or going somewhere that everyone wants to go are some ideas. Try tying these activities into some recognizable event, such as a birthday or holiday.

I suspect that my daughter may be cutting herself. What should I do?
First, you need to understand that this is another sign of a fragile identity in the works. Reading Chapter 6 again to get a clear picture

of the differences between *fragile* and *resilient* identities is a good place to start. Once you identify which characteristics of a fragile identity best describe your teenager, you will be in a better position to decide what to do. Second, don't be too quick to seek medication as an answer. Your teen may indeed be depressed, but that depression may stem from an identity crisis, not some chemical imbalance. In addition, getting a psychiatric diagnosis isn't usually the best way to boost a teen's self-esteem! Instead, do a lot of listening and try to get a sense of how your teen sees the world. What issues confront her? Is bullying an issue? Does she feel like an outsider, or defective in some way? Does she feel successful in some areas, and effective in getting at least some things that are important? What options for adult life does she perceive are available? If you can put a name to your teen's emerging identity, you can then turn to any of the guidelines presented in this book to help create experiences that will give her fresh perspective on life and what her options are.

How can I begin to introduce spirituality into my teen's life and identity?

Spirituality has to do with the way we live our lives. You can definitely identify spiritual versus nonspiritual lifestyles (see the chart in Chapter 10). One way to begin to introduce spirituality into your family's day-to-day life is by expressing *gratitude*. Being capable of feeling gratitude for what you have is one aspect of being a spiritual person. There are many ways to do this. One example is establishing a family ritual of saying grace before every meal. You can also express gratitude in many other ways. The critical thing is to make a point of expressing gratitude for something on a regular basis. The opposite of gratitude is envy. Chronic envy leads to a state of chronic resentment and can contribute to self-defeating alienation in your teen. Therefore, avoid expressing envy. Learn to catch yourself when you feel envious and think instead of something that you are grateful for.

What role does my relationship with my teen play in promoting spirituality?

It plays a critical role and can have a major impact on your teen's emerging identity. The extent to which you value your *relationships* as much as you value status or material *possessions* and your *social status* is a measure of how much you are living a spiritual lifestyle. Again, our culture encourages us to measure our worth using yardsticks such as the kind of car we drive or house we live in, or our job title. It's easy to see teens buying into this and valuing themselves according to what brand of clothing they wear or what kind of cell phone they carry. Now consider how important these things are to *you*. Can you honestly say that the quality of your relationships with your partner, your children, and your friends is as important or more important than your status? The more you can work toward achieving this for yourself, the more evident it will become to your teen, and the more he or she is likely to incorporate it into his or her identity.

What does generosity have to do with spirituality?

Generosity is another facet of spirituality. Doing something for others or contributing to others in need helps us to feel we have a purpose in living other than simply acquiring and consuming things. We can be generous with our money; but we can also be generous with our *time*. Many times, the latter has more impact on others than the former. Our society promotes self-centeredness—in adults as well as teens—much more than it advocates charity. Establishing a family tradition of occasional service work, making teens aware of any money you contribute to charity, and just plain sharing something with someone else are all ways that you can model a spiritual lifestyle. Spirituality also represents ideas to believe in, and making your ideas known to your teenager is important to identity development.

What is interdependency and how does it relate to spirituality?
First, there is nothing wrong with being able to take care of your-self, set your own goals, and learn to overcome adversity through perseverance, if that's what you mean by being independent. On the other hand, if what you mean by independent is being an island unto yourself, that's not an ideal worth pursuing. A spiritual person is someone who is capable of standing on his or her own two feet, but who also feels part of a larger group—a family, a community and is willing to work in concert with others to achieve common goals. A good example is the old tradition of barn raising, in which an entire community would gather together to build a barn. In this way, every family farm would have its own barn, all of which were built through shared labor.

If you think of your family and your community in that light—with each individual being capable, but also needing to work together at times—you will build interdependency. One way to do this is to approach some tasks as family projects. For example, build a family garden, put up or paint a fence together, or delegate the tasks necessary to pack up for the family vacation. Avoid as much as possible creating a family environment in which each individual is doing his or her thing separately, without much interdependence. This will help you steer your teen toward an identity that is less likely to lead to isolation, an identity better able to reach out to others in times of crisis.

INDEX

ABOUT THE AUTHOR

Joseph Nowinski, Ph.D., has held positions as Assistant Professor of Psychiatry at the University of California San Francisco, and Associate Adjunct Professor of Psychology at the University of Connecticut. His previous books include *Substance Abuse in Adolescents and Young Adults: A Guide to Treatment, The Tender Heart: Conquering Your Insecurity*, and *Six Questions That Can Change Your Life*. Dr. Nowinski consults to universities and treatment facilities, and speaks frequently to parent groups on issues related to adolescent development and treatment. He started the first residential treatment facility in Connecticut dedicated to helping teenagers with alcohol and drug problems. He has worked with families and adolescents in private practice, residential treatment, and correctional facilities. He lives with his family in Tolland, Connecticut. Dr. Nowinski welcomes questions and comments about his books. He can be reached at JNowinski@sbcglobal.net.